"Mike Woodruff has written a book that belong[s] those who are managerially challenged, he through the day and through the event. Fo[r] provided a resource that can take a person to the next level in leadership and management. Mike has combined his years in youth ministry with the knowledge and experience he's gained as a management consultant to produce a book that is practical, humorous, inspirational, biblical, and significant."

Denny Rydberg
President of Young Life

"For years 'youth ministry' and 'organizational management' have been mortal enemies. Though used as a joke for some, and a badge of pride for others, the tendency of youth workers to be seen in most churches as last-minute 'wing-it' delayed adolescents has ultimately hurt our ministry to students. Mike Woodruff, the long-recognized leading voice in youth ministry organization, management, and strategy, has produced a landmark book for addressing this issue. This is a great book, one that I believe needs to be read and reread by every youth worker."

Chap Clark
Professor of Youth and Family Ministries at Fuller Theological Seminary

"Youth workers can choose from lots of books on leadership, but few books on management are as helpful, user friendly, or fun to read as this one."

Bill Clem
National Director of Student Ministries, SonLife

"Like it or not, youth ministers are managers of organizations. Youth work requires special knowledge for developing staff, resolving conflicts, creating programs, and generating long-term plans. Here's a *good* book to provide guidance in all these tasks."

Tony Campolo
Eastern College
St. Davids, Pennsylvania

Managing Youth Ministry Chaos by Mike Woodruff

Loveland, Colorado

Dedication

To my wife, who quietly and effectively practices what I preach.

Visit our Web site: **www.grouppublishing.com**

Credits
Book Acquisitions Editor: Amy Simpson
Editor: Debbie Gowensmith
Quality Control Editor: Jim Kochenburger
Chief Creative Officer: Joani Schultz
Copy Editor: Betty Taylor
Art Director: Jean Bruns
Cover Art Director: Jeff A. Storm
Cover Designer: Cathy Maners
Computer Graphic Artist: Pat Miller
Cartoonist: Mike Woodruff
Production Manager: Peggy Naylor

Unless otherwise noted, Scripture taken from the HOLY BIBLE, NEW INTERNATIONAL VERSION®. Copyright © 1973, 1978, 1984 by International Bible Society. Used by permission of Zondervan Publishing House. All rights reserved.

Library of Congress Cataloging-in-Publication Data
Woodruff, Mike, 1960-
    Managing youth ministry chaos / by Mike Woodruff.
        p.   cm.
    Includes index.
    ISBN 0-7644-2143-3 (alk. paper)
    1. Church work with youth. 2. Church youth workers.
    3. Management--Religious aspects--Christianity. I. Title.
    BV4447.W66 2000
    254--dc21   99-44725
                                           CIP

10 9 8 7 6 5 4 3 2 1   09 08 07 06 05 04 03 02 01 00

Printed in the United States of America.

Management Tips

Youth pastors are a unique breed, and our pace of life and occupational quirks prove it. Our offices mix books and computers with Frisbees, water cannons, rock videos, and boxes of pancake batter mix. We gravitate toward lateness—as in stay up late, show up late, and grow up late. And we thrive on action. In fact, chaperoning white-water rafting trips is how we relax.

But put us in a real office, make us wear starchy dress clothes and attend long planning meetings, give us a job that starts to look like…well…a job, and some of us go ballistic. We don't do the organization thing. It's not our shtick.

For a long time, I thought that was OK. Kids aren't organized, so why should we be? But now I'm singing a different song. Why should we accept messy desks, missed meetings, and marathon workweeks as part of our routine when few other professionals do? Why are we so quick to accept our stereotype as energetic but unorganized, spiritual but messy, well-intentioned but misdirected, when it really is a backhanded put-down?

The more I think about it, the more reasons I see to distance ourselves from our reputation. That won't be easy, but we can start by understanding that our chaos is legitimate. We have good reasons for approaching work the way we do.

• **We know no other way.** Many people begin their youth ministries without any formal training. Others begin after a few years at Christian colleges or seminaries, where they weren't given much exposure to the real issues they'll face. I spent three years studying Greek, Hebrew, postexilic prophets, and the finer points of economic Trinitarianism, but somehow I managed to miss the course on how to take a youth group to Mexico.

Many of us make the job look difficult—as if it *requires* long hours and a Herculean effort—because we don't really know what we're doing. Many of us push papers from one pile to another simply because we don't know where to put them. Many of us appear unorganized because we are. We've learned what we know about management from watching other people do a poor job.

• **We have too much freedom.** Many youth ministers fail because they have too long a leash. Think about it: With the exception of Wednesday nights and Sunday mornings, who really knows where you are or what you're up to? Vice presidents of Fortune 500 companies have less autonomy at age fifty-five than we do at age twenty-three. And with the exception of the senior pastor and church secretary, almost no one is around to hold us accountable. Granted, some youth ministers use their freedom wisely. But for everyone who does, a dozen flounder. We overschedule, run late to meetings, or procrastinate. We lack the wisdom and discipline to manage our time well.

We face other hurdles as well. Our job never really ends—short of our students' graduation or our graves—we lack the proper support staff and equipment, we're often wired to respond instead of lead, and so on. You get the point. Few youth ministers are prepared to manage the chaos they face. And because of this, many ministries are less successful than they could be.

In fact, most are. If I were a betting man, I'd wager the family farm that it is not desire, effort, or opportunity that limits most youth ministries. It's leadership. And more specifically, it's managerial leadership. The truth is that you can't grow a ministry beyond your ability to manage it. The chaos wins.

And so I offer you *Managing Youth Ministry Chaos*. It actually was not my idea. Like most other things I've worked on, I borrowed the concept from someone brighter than myself. In this case, that person was the late Robert Townsend, past chairman of the Avis car rental company and noted corporate iconoclast. His books *Up the Organization* and *Further Up the Organization* were as close to Dilbert as management thinkers came in the 1970s. I loved *Up the Organization* from the moment I stumbled across it because Townsend's wit and insight were married to such a simple format that the book was actually fun to read. (I'd originally hoped simply to photocopy large sections of his work, change a few illustrations, and claim it as my own for *Managing Youth Ministry Chaos*. But apparently Group Publishing is a bit more concerned about copyright laws than most youth pastors.)

So have at it. Pick up the book, and start reading anywhere. Look for one or two management tips, arranged alphabetically, that you can put into practice right now. Feel free to disagree with me about any point; management isn't an exact science. Just don't set the thing down on your desk, or it will get buried under the pancake batter mix, the volleyball net, and your eighteen-page to-do list. You won't be able to find it again and will have to go out and buy another copy. (On the other hand, set the book down wherever you'd like!)

After-Action Reports

Every youth pastor who has survived a calendar change can profit from a simple management tool called the after-action report (AAR). Here's an example to show you how it works. This year as you get ready for the annual ski retreat—reserving the vans, booking the speaker, publicizing the retreat, and so on—jot down what you do and when you do it as you go. After the retreat, spend five minutes thinking about what went right, what went wrong, and what you would do differently if you could do it over. Then type your notes as a timetable—for example, "Four weeks before the retreat, I did A, B, and C. Two weeks before the retreat, I did D, E, and F. The day of the retreat, I did G, H, and I." Finally, place the notes in a file to use next time.

Then when you plan another ski retreat, take out the AAR, hand it to Billy Bob, and say, "B.B., it's all yours. See you on the slopes." Billy Bob plans the retreat and then adds his insights to the AAR. If he needs more planning help, you can use the AAR to guide your delegation.

You can—and should—draft an AAR for any reoccurring event. Over the years, these AARs will become so helpful that you'll be fired and the entire program will be turned over to a chimpanzee, who will be paid only slightly more than you are today.

Bad-Mouthing Predecessors, or Knocking the Nose Off the Sphinx

We've all seen pictures of the Great Sphinx of Giza, that wonderful Egyptian monument parked next to the Pyramids. It has the body of a 240-foot lion, the head of a man, and a panoramic view of the surrounding desert. What it doesn't have, though, is a nose. Why? Because someone knocked it off. Sphinxes were made in the images of kings, but many are without noses because the succeeding kings ordered the statues defaced—often as one of their first acts of power (Steven W. G. Moore, Ph.D., in an unpublished paper titled "Ending Well, Starting Well").

Five thousand years later, we see the vandals as weak and self-centered bureaucrats, not legendary leaders. Yet most of us knock off a few noses ourselves. How? By bad-mouthing our predecessors, by listening to others do the same, or by unnecessarily dismantling our predecessors' work.

• **Speaking ill of others.** Unless you're forwarding your predecessors' mail to the state prison (and even then it's best to keep quiet), you shouldn't say anything bad about them. You gain nothing by tearing down their memory; those who disliked them are unlikely to dislike them more, and those who esteem them will only think less of you.

• **Listening to others talk trash.** Under the cover of "There are a few things I think you should know…"or "I really like what you're doing because it's so much more helpful than…" well-intentioned people—and a few ill-intentioned as well—will try to talk ill of your predecessors. Don't go there. If you sense they have a legitimate need to talk about their disappointments with the past, ask them to tell you about their needs that were not met. After listening carefully, you've won the right to say,"I believe my predecessors, even though they weren't perfect, were God's choice for this job back then. I'm not in a position to know about what did or didn't happen, but let me tell you what I hope to do."

• **Dismantling their work.** I'm on record as an advocate of change, but let me be clear: Good change is not change for change's sake and certainly is not change to discredit your predecessors. Celebrate their successes. When you find it necessary to deep-six one of their programs, do so with class. Explain that the program was great during its time but is no longer the best option. Or instead of dropping the program, launch a new venture alongside it. That may provide a graceful transition from the old program to the new and may keep you from making enemies of those not quite ready to part with the past. Whatever you do, don't take down a fence until you know why it was put up.

Boss-Bashing

Boss-bashing is common practice in this country. In fact, it's so popular that some magazines have "worst boss of the year" contests. People submit reasons why their employers are the biggest morons on the planet, and they hope to win a prize for doing so.

While most youth pastors would never stoop that low, at least formally, we often engage in a practice just as harmful without ever intending to. We circulate among people who actually condemn our boss with their faint praise—for example, "Pastor Bob does a pretty good job, all things considered," or "As a person I think Pastor Bob is wonderful, but as a pastor…" What makes these conversations so difficult to avoid is that they usually begin with comments like "Boy, we sure do wish you would preach more; you have such a gift," or "We know it's not Pastor Bob's fault, but he just doesn't have the people skills you do," or "If the church had the kind of leadership you've offered the youth group, everything would be just fine."

Neutral parties see these comments for what they are—bait for a trap. But it's difficult for us to think straight when we finally meet someone who sees our tremendous potential. Nevertheless, if you want an effective working relationship with your senior pastor, you have to be loyal.

My advice is that when you hear anything resembling, "He means well, but we're

"Yeah, it could have been gang members, but I still think it was the youth pastor."

11

sure you'd do better," it's time to take action. Option 1 is to run—not walk—to the nearest exit; do not pass go or collect two hundred dollars. Option 2 is to confront the person making the comment: "I'm not sure I agree with you, Gene. As part of the staff, I see things from a different perspective. But if you have some criticisms, why don't you talk directly to Pastor Bob? I think he'd profit from hearing what you think." Do take action, though. The last thing you can afford to be is the unwitting pawn in a power play by disgruntled church members.

Budgets

Most youth pastors know more about popular music than they do about budgeting. This is a nice way of saying that when it comes to financial savvy, we are dog paddling in the shallow end of the gene pool. And though this may not seem like such a big deal to you—hey, we don't have much money to mishandle—we probably should be less willy-nilly with dollars and cents than say…oh…Congress.

In the interest of full disclosure, I must note that I made some big financial errors in my rookie season. Once while making a financial report designed to instill some confidence in my fiscal management abilities, an elder pointed out that absolutely none of my columns added up. Not one. The elder then proceeded to ask me a whole series of basic questions that I couldn't answer. On another occasion, shortly after some wishful projections led us to prematurely add a second college pastor, a member of my board took me aside and said, "Mike, if a businessperson made the same mistake you just did, he'd go under. And yet somehow—under the guise of faith or spirituality—you think you can just come back to us and ask for more money."

Ouch.

I could fill page after page with stories of youth pastors who were so cavalier in their approach to finances that they not only lost money, but also their jobs. But that would only lead some of you to assume that you're not as bad as most people. So instead let me be clear: You do not break the laws of finance. The laws of finance break you.

• **Recruit help.** Some people live for numbers. They enjoy credits and debits. They dream about spreadsheets and general ledgers. They even read Accounting Digest and attend workshops on fiscal control. Fifteen years ago, you beat them up on the playground. Let's hope they've forgotten, because now you need their help. I know many of you would rather chew sand than invite a number cruncher to review your check register, but you've got no choice. Sooner or later someone in the church is going to demand an internal audit. And speaking from experience, it's better to ask for help now instead of then. Invite a bean counter to help you set up a good fiscal system.

• **Understand your church.** Some churches have budgets that read like a

John Grisham novel (i.e., legal fiction) and should be printed in red ink. Other churches have such tight fiscal control that they'd give God a receipt for manna. You need to know which kind of church you're working for and adapt your style accordingly—especially at the former. There's a big difference between a budget and actual spendable capital. Just because the church leaders approve a $22,000 line item for youth ministry doesn't mean you'll see the money. Youth budgets are not immune to the ax, especially in churches that implement across-the-board cuts. Develop a positive working relationship with the church treasurer. Keep him or her posted on your current and upcoming needs. If you keep separate books, be sure to reconcile yours with theirs—as well as the bank's—on a monthly basis. Additionally, ask for advice on the church's budgeting system.

• **Buy software.** For two or three hundred dollars, you can buy a basic software program designed for people who can't even find their checkbooks, let alone balance them. These user-friendly packages—Microsoft Profit and Intuit's Quicken are two of the most popular—will force you to account for every penny. They will help you print out financial reports that make you look like you know what you're doing. Just be sure to back up your data, and read the owners manual.

• **Draft a budget.** Create a plan for how you will spend the money. Use last year's check register to help you figure out where the money went. Then make some adjustments based on this year's programming calendar, and draft an outline of your projected spending for the upcoming year. Budgets not only help you monitor expenses versus income on a year-to-date basis, but they also help you realize the true cost of an event. After all, just because you have money left over at the end of a retreat doesn't mean you made a profit. The true cost of the event includes the two-hundred-dollar deposit you made nine months ago and many other ancillary expenses you have probably forgotten about.

• **Conduct internal audits.** Every so often someone from the church should be given free license to snoop around the books and to ask lots and lots of questions. This audit will likely uncover unwise practices—for example, my habit of taking the offering home in my pocket—and lead to a battery of suggestions. Follow them. Audits not only assure other people that the money is being well handled, but also provide you with a measure of protection. In fact, you should request an internal audit at least every other year.

• **Embrace profit.** Some ministers seem to think the church's nonprofit status prohibits them from making a profit on anything. Others apparently think it is morally wrong for any type of youth event to finish in the black. I happen to think just the opposite. Events should break even or make money. If they don't, I want to know why. Try to run a youth ministry program that supports itself.

Calendars

You should have one and only one calendar, and you should carry it with you at all times. This means the calendar should be either small or electronic or both. When the church mails out a newsletter, complete with a calendar of events, copy what matters to you onto your calendar, and throw the rest away. Do the same with your soccer team schedule and any and every other collection of times and dates that people hand to you. To avoid losing your mind, make a photocopy or backup of this calendar at least once a week.

Change Management

We are living in a world of chaos and change. Much has been written on the topic. It's a good idea for you to understand at least the basics.

• **Organizations must change.** Jack Welch, the legendary CEO of GE, noted, "If the change inside an institution does not match the change outside of it, then the end of that institution is in sight." Welch was not talking about the church and is not qualified to. After all, some of what we hold onto in the church must never change. However, Welch's point is worth pondering. The tactics you employed to build your ministry are possibly the same tactics that could spell its demise. In fact,

At the Rocket Science Lab

"Look Johnson, you don't have to be a youth pastor to figure this out."

nothing characterizes successful organizations more than their willingness to abandon what made them successful.

• **Know what is eternal.** With the exception of small children in dirty diapers, some church members will not want to see anything changed. Nothing. Nada. Zip, zilch, and zero. Don't make the opposite mistake. As a Christian leader, you must help define the future. Knowing what part of the present to protect is an absolutely critical first step.

• **People own what they create.** If you want to institute organizational change, you must include the people in the process. People own what they create and fight what is forced upon them. Furthermore, the more input people have in a process, the more they will fight for its success. In other words, my idea might be 20 percent better than your idea, but you'll work one hundred times harder to make sure your idea works.

• **Emotions are the crux of the matter.** It's not the physical process of change that trips us up; we can quickly learn to make those kinds of adjustments. And it's seldom the intellectual modifications that stump us; we can learn how to use new software, fill out new tax forms, or speak a new language. The challenges we face are emotional. Change is overwhelming, and we often don't feel up to it. This is even truer today, when so many people are weary of change. The number of changes they face, the magnitude of each change, and the lack of time between changes have all accelerated. The net result is that change feels exponential. People may even be coming to the church hoping to find a place that isn't going to change.

• **Change when the wind is in your sails.** The time to tack in a sailboat is when you have enough speed to make the switch; if you wait too long before you turn, you stall. The time to change an organization is when the old ways are still working. If you wait until you are losing momentum, you've waited too long.

• **Change takes time.** Some people resist anything new, and they'll go to their graves defending the traditions they embraced as a child. A second group will resist change for a while but will warm to it over time. If you ask, or force, people in this second group to take a public stand before they've had enough time to process the new idea, they're likely to stick with what they know. If you fight them over their decision, their pride may prevent them from ever changing to your side.

• **Be aware of the relationship between anxiety 1 and 2.** In order for people to change, the aversion to change—which I'll call anxiety 1—must be *less than* the aversion to remain the same—which I'll call anxiety 2. Think of it this way: The main reason some people learn to snowboard is because their fear of being a social pariah—*What dude, you don't board?*—is greater than their fear of racing down a mountain with both feet cemented to a four-foot plank. Since some people would rather squeeze poison from a python than be labeled a coward, they'll always try something new. Whereas other people—think of them as the best skiers on the hill—don't see much value in trading something they're great at for something they do poorly. Their anxiety 1 is greater than their anxiety 2, and they will resist change. Good leaders seek ways to lower anxiety 1 in people before they resort to raising anxiety 2.

• **Don't confuse a general desire to change with support for your plan.** When things are going poorly, everyone is excited about change. Even people who have never agreed with you might appear to be on your side. Be careful. Don't confuse their dislike of the present situation with support for your vision. The first is easy to come by; the second, much more difficult.

• **Recognize the personal toll.** Finally, understand that leading change is personally taxing. Organizations do not change willingly. They have survived and grown in part because of their ability to protect the status quo. Agents of change pay a high toll on the highway toward the future. Sometimes they get run over. Choose wisely the situations for which you are willing to become road kill.

Choosing Your Battles

In our profession, it's easy to take a stand on everything from the deity of Christ to the color of paint in the youth room. Be careful. Not everything is important. Do not be sanctimonious. Do choose carefully the battles you're willing to fight. Church history is littered with the bodies of youth pastors who chose poorly and died over nonessentials.

Church Leader Meetings

You need a driver's license to operate a car but no qualifications to call a meeting, which means any fool can do so. You're bound to suffer folly in meetings—especially church leader meetings, which have been known to last through several presidential administrations. However, if you're asked to attend, do two things: Secure a specific time on the agenda, and prepare for your part. The reason for the first is simple: You don't want to listen to five or ten or twelve people debate about which type of lawn mower the church should buy. These discussions can go on for hours, and it's rude to lie down on the floor and go to sleep. The reason for the second is also clear: Because the church leadership is unlikely to hang out at *your* meetings, your reports to them are just about all they know of your work. Think about it. With the exception of visibly helping on Sunday mornings and preaching once or twice a year, the only time this group sees you in action is at its meetings. This means you'd better do well.

College Prep

How much of what you do today will matter in fifteen years? ten percent? twenty? seventy-five? It's a sobering question, but one we'd better ask. Because while we're great with activities—name one other profession that promotes banana madness parties and sumo wrestling contests—they don't count. Results do. And our results aren't pretty.

There is a black hole the size of Montana that swallows about 70 percent of our graduating seniors. They look, smell, and act as if they have a viable faith right up until they saunter into their first class at the university. Then, virtually overnight, they morph into the crowd on an MTV spring-break video—or worse.

Which leaves us with two options. We can spend a lot of time debating whether they ever were Christians, or we can analyze our approach.

While making no claims to omniscience, on at least two occasions, I've tried something besides whining. Along with a handful of other people, I took to the college campus to track down Christian college students who had two things in common: (1) They had been active in a high school youth group and (2) they were still following Christ after their freshman year in college.

The question we set out to answer was, "What did your youth pastor do right?" (You should try the same drill.) Here's what we found.

• **They taught kids to think.** A naive and simplistic faith is about as useful as last semester's meal ticket. Students need the ability to think for themselves. A few pat answers and some rote memory verses will carry them through about ten minutes of their first college class. And let's face it: There are some very difficult questions out there that we don't have answers to. If the first person to point this out to your students is their psychology professor instead of you, then they'll be toast by Thanksgiving. Introduce high school seniors to the kinds of dilemmas they'll face at the U. Suggest hypothetical situations, and allow them to role play scenarios they're likely to face. At all costs, teach them how to find the answers they need, and assure them that God doesn't depend on their ability to answer every objection thrown their way.

• **They helped their students become independently dependent on God.** Everyone wants college freshmen. Clubs want them to become members, marketing execs want them to buy their companies' products, hall councils want them to run for office, and professors want them to study. Everywhere college freshmen turn, they face competition for their time. As a result, they run in ninety-three directions when they can only manage twenty-five. Among the things that suffer is their personal time with Christ. Skip the guilt sessions and threats, but work hard to make daily time in the Book a part of their most basic makeup.

• **They stressed Christian community.** The students whose faith survives the first ten minutes of fall semester have something else in common—Christian friends. These students have learned how to transfer the support they received from youth leaders and youth groups to relationships with believing college peers. University fellowships are natural places to find these friends. In fact, one theme we heard from survivors is that their youth pastors or parents did more than tell them to get plugged in to a church; they made sure it happened. Some youth pastors called the colleges to find out about active Christian groups, then arranged for meetings between their students and the leaders of those groups. Other youth pastors loaded everyone into a van and actually went to campus to help kids make the transition.

Computers

Technology isn't foolproof; it doesn't protect us from our own foibles. Things will go wrong on the high-tech frontier, so take precautions.

• **Back it up.** This one step will prevent most of your technology headaches. I try to back up my files once a week. Keep these files off-site so in the event of a fire or flood, you won't lose both copies of your data.

• **Get insurance.** Many church insurance policies do not cover personal property. If you own the computer that sits on your desk in the church office, it's probably

When pastors use spellcheckers

"And if you have an unshaved friend they need to hear about the good spell."

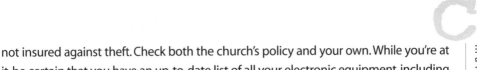

not insured against theft. Check both the church's policy and your own. While you're at it, be certain that you have an up-to-date list of all your electronic equipment, including serial numbers, software, upgrades, and so on. This information is crucial if you need to make a claim.

• **Use a surge protector.** A power surge can blow your computer's chip in a nanosecond, so be sure you have a working surge protector. Note: Some protectors self-destruct in the line of duty, and you can't always tell when they have done so. Test them periodically, and replace them if they fail. Better yet, when the storm clouds roll across the horizon, unplug your machines.

• **Watch the dust.** Everyone knows that electronic equipment doesn't like water, but you should realize that it also doesn't handle dust well either. In fact, many machines fail because dust forms an electric arc and shorts out the machines. Be honest—just how long has it been since anyone has taken a dust rag to your office?

• **Clean your hard drive.** Periodically delete all your old files. This will not only make your current files easier to find, but will also speed up your hard drive. But don't stop there. Computer shops sell disk drive cleaners. They resemble tape and video cleaners and can add some life to your machine. Once a month run the cleaning disk through your floppy drive.

Conference Calls

You choose.

Option 1: Leave home at 6:30 p.m., set up a room at the church, meet for forty-five minutes—thirty of which is extraneous—clean up the room, drive home. Elapsed time: ninety minutes.

Option 2: Stay home. At 6:55 p.m., place phone calls to network the participants. Begin the conference call promptly at 7 p.m. Because there is some expense involved—although given current rate wars, not much—people get to the point. At 7:15, hang up. No travel time, no cleanup, no night away from family.

Control

Our control falls under four types of events:

1. Events we believe we can't control and, in fact, we can't control them—the weather, for example.

2. Events we believe we can't control when, in fact, we can control them—a reoccurring emergency, for example.

3. Events we believe we can control when, in fact, we can't control them—other people's responses, for example.

4. Events we know we can control but for some reason don't control—personal organization, for example.

We need to write off numbers one and three and to focus our attention on numbers two and four. To do otherwise is to fret, stress, and waste time.

Creativity

Being wild, loud, and immature—albeit with professional license—is not the same thing as being creative. In fact, there is nothing very novel about hosting a forty-eight-hour Sumo-Wrestling Jamboree when forty-three other groups have done exactly the same thing.

So while I'll admit that youth ministers are, as a rule, more creative than accountants, who end up in jail if they get too novel, the problem is that youth ministers—you—don't develop their creativity. We generally don't know how.

Corporate America, which is setting and following business trends more fanatically than teenage girls are setting and following fashion trends, is moving into creativity training in a big way. Daunted by the magnitude of changes they face, one set of strategists believes that the only way forward is with breakthrough thinking. Consequently businesses are trying to help their employees recapture some of the free form they enjoyed before society squeezed them into the classroom. Much of the training is ballyhoo and tommyrot. But some of the suggestions are worth acting upon.

• **Define the problem.** Don't expect clever ideas to pop into your head (it's not that porous). Instead, select a problem, and then rigorously define it. The creative process works best when sandwiched between periods of careful analysis.

• **Ask "why?" and "what if?" questions at least ten times each day.** "Why do we meet on Wednesday nights?" "Why do we meet at the church?" "Why don't we have sixty-year-olds in our group?" "What if we spent a month in Mexico instead of a week?" "What if we didn't have to worry about money at all?" "What if we could hold our meetings during lunch break at the high school?"

• **Spend time with people who are successful in other fields.** Learn how journalists, scientists, and tugboat captains solve problems. Look for approaches in their worlds that are novel in yours, or invite them to help you brainstorm. Because they know nothing about the way you typically approach things, they may discover quick wins.

• **Rescue success from failure.** Desperation is a great creativity catalyst. Case in point: Federal Express was established to fly cash around the country for the Federal Reserve Bank. But when the bank turned down the idea, Fred Smith was left with two idle jets and a lot of debt. He turned to delivering packages—and was successful beyond his wildest hopes—only because he had to.

- **Read books about creativity.** Don't read the flaky stuff that promotes navel gazing and fun with Play-Doh. Instead study some serious contributions to the field. Edward deBono, a Rhodes Scholar and international consulting wonder, is one guru. His book *Six Thinking Hats* is probably the best place to start. Roger Von Oech's contributions—both his books and his Creative Whack Pack—are also good introductions.

- **Force yourself to discover multiple solutions.** Most of us never get a chance to be creative because we apply the first promising idea that comes along. Force yourself to generate a list of ten to twelve possible options. Keep looking at a problem until you have a dozen viable—and novel—solutions to choose from.

- **Learn a new skill.** I recently took up oil painting. It's a new world for me, and consequently I'm learning not only about colors, canvas, and lighting, but also about observation. I see lots of things differently because of the skills I'm learning from painting.

Crises

Murphy's Law has a daunting number of subsets, and you will likely learn them all. If something can go wrong, it will—at the worst time, at the worst place. And somehow or another, it will involve the pastor's daughter or a church leader's son or, in worst-case scenarios, both of them. In other words, there are two stages to youth ministry: crisis and precrisis. You either deal with trouble or prepare for it.

Of course not all your problems are bona fide crises. Some are simply headaches common to a fallen world; those problems, you try to avoid or handle on the fly. You prepare for the major problems because how you respond in a real fire may not only determine your employment status, but may also save a life.

- **Employ preventive defense.** The best way to deal with a crisis is to avoid it. In fact, that's what you're paid to do. Granted, some emergencies are utterly unforeseeable. But most are not. And if you're blindsided by an event, it should never happen twice. For example, it's acceptable to have your files ruined by a flood in the church basement. But it is not OK for it to happen again the following year.

- **Make contingency plans.** Businesses draft contingency plans for their more likely or more foreboding disasters. The process is not as cumbersome as it sounds and really amounts to little more than collecting a handful of reasonably bright people and asking, "What should we do if this happens?" By dealing with these events before they occur, you avoid the mental fog and panic that a real crisis causes. Take five minutes at your next staff meeting to talk about the following questions:
  - What would we do if we lost the van keys while we were in Mexico?
  - What if our outreach speaker canceled at the last minute?

- What if a student got lost on a trip?
- How would we get medical help during our rafting trip?
- What if our computers crashed and we lost all our files?
- What if the church catches fire during a Sunday morning service?

Routinely ask these kinds of questions while planning any major event, especially if you're leaving the country or are planning to be away from main roads. Five minutes of foresight can save you hours of headaches and hassles.

- **Keep your head.** After preventing a crisis, defining one is the most important step. The nature of our work puts us around a lot of young and often immature people—just the type to inflate an incident by prescribing a tourniquet for a paper cut. These people are called "amplifiers." You must be a deflator. And take note: Hysteria spreads on secondhand information. Don't let people blow things out of proportion.

Get the facts. Do everything you can to confirm details.

Share accurate information. In the absence of specific details, people pass along rumors. If you don't have all the information you'd like, share that—for example, "This is what has happened. We know XYZ. We're waiting to find out ABC. When we know more, we'll tell you. Right now, this is all anybody knows for sure. Lesser people would walk away from this and start spreading more rumors. I need to rely on you not to do that."

Seek expert advice. The longer I live, the more value I find in calling church leaders "elders." People who have lived through a handful of crises can help you keep things in perspective.

Take action, action, action. Assuming that you're dealing with a legitimate crisis, avoid the common tendency of wasting time assigning blame. The people who messed up already know it, and there will be plenty of time to debrief later. Fix the problem.

Take prudent action. At the same time, you must also realize that your first thoughts are seldom the best. Avoid the urge to "just do something," and take at least sixty seconds to formulate a plan. More than one person has run to call for help only to later learn that someone had a cell phone right there. Huddle with one or two other people to draft a plan. "What's the next step?" "Who can we call for advice?" The bigger the crisis, the more important it is to bring the senior pastor and church leaders into the loop as soon as possible. They will help you form a crisis management team. Note: Always carry the phone numbers for your must-reach people.

- **Act after the crisis.** After the immediate situation has settled down, a second set of questions needs to be addressed with your crisis management team.

Handle the press. Good news doesn't ever seem to find its way into the local paper, but bad news usually will—and quickly. If the crisis is serious, you should prepare for a call from a reporter. Draft a statement, and have someone with some

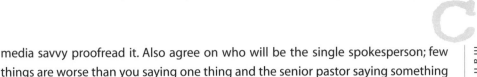

media savvy proofread it. Also agree on who will be the single spokesperson; few things are worse than you saying one thing and the senior pastor saying something else. Inform everyone to defer questions to the spokesperson. You don't have to answer every question a reporter asks—in fact, it's usually legally dangerous to do so—but never lie or say "no comment." One is bad, and the other almost always makes you look bad.

Contact legal counsel. In this day and age, you should expect to be sued, especially if you are at fault. Hold-harmless forms (see p. 45) can help, but they won't prevent suits. In the event of a major disaster, ask the church board to retain an attorney. Many churches have legal counsel. Others rely on attorneys from their membership roles. If you are insured, also contact the insurance company immediately. Not only is the company likely to assign a staff attorney to your case, but an insurance investigator will likely rush to the scene.

Provide counseling. With all the attention going to meet the needs of an injured student—or an accident victim's family members—be sure someone pays attention to the emotional needs of the rest of the group. Many therapists are trained to offer just this type of support. When a counselor drowned at a Christian camp on the West Coast, one phone call was all it took to recruit an entire battery of counselors trained to help the survivors deal with their grief and pain. Following a rock-climbing fatality, a church's entire sanctuary was filled with pastors, psychiatrists, and psychologists ready to counsel students. The church's board agreed to cover the counselors' initial expenses and any long-term therapy costs for students most closely related to the accident.

Debrief. In the days or weeks following a crisis, gather the leadership team and others who may be able to help, and review the event. What could have been done to prevent the accident? Could it have been predicted? Knowing what we now know, how could we have dealt with the situation more effectively? Were we properly insured? Should we change any church policies?

Criticism—Giving

Sometime during your ministry, you will need to criticize others. This is not a skill seminaries teach. And seldom is the first thing out of your mouth the best. Fortunately, constructive criticism is a skill we can improve. Here are some suggestions:

• **Consider your objective.** Why do you want to criticize this person? Is your goal to punish or to help him or her improve? Are you angry? Are you trying to get even? Do you genuinely want what is best for this person? Constructive criticism is ultimately about building people up, not tearing them down. You need to begin with a level head. Remember, it is not always wrong to criticize someone in anger, but it is wrong to criticize someone before you've had a chance to look objectively at the situation. What is your objective?

- **Write an outline of your comments.** Few things are worse than vague attacks, so be certain you can be specific. Write an outline of the one or two items you need to discuss. (Keep short accounts with people so you don't need to bring up more than two items per discussion.) Be sure you focus on behavior the person can change. Consider opening with a positive comment about his or her performance before you focus on the concerns.

- **Consider the time and place.** The ideal time to criticize is as close to the event as possible, but this doesn't always work out. For example, if someone is very tired or discouraged, it might be prudent to delay your remarks. Also remember that you can praise in public but you should criticize only in private.

- **Don't break the rules.** There are no rules in a knockdown, drag-out, winner-take-all fight. But in the give-and-take of constructive criticism, there are rules:

    Criticize the work, not the worker. Don't say, "You're stupid because…" Do say, "Spray painting the pastor's car was not a smart thing to do."

    Do not overstate. Never say "never" and always avoid "always" because you never need to use them and they always cause trouble.

    Do not keep repeating the same point. It's stupid to repeat the same point. People get bored if you repeat the same point. If you simply say the same thing again and again, you look as if you don't have anything else to say. Besides, repetition is boring.

    Do not use sarcasm. Enough said.

- **Don't lecture. Have a conversation.** I learned early on that I seldom have all the facts straight even when I'm sure I do. State your case, and then ask for feedback. The truth probably lies somewhere between what you're thinking and what the other person is thinking.

- **Agree on the next step.** If you're criticizing someone's work performance, you must be certain that everyone leaves the session very clear about who will do what next. It may be helpful to set up a time for follow-up or a deadline for change.

- **Do not apologize.** If the criticism is constructive and your motives are pure, apologizing weakens your credibility.

Criticism—Receiving

It's a good thing you're reading this section because you're one of the most incompetent and inconsiderate also-rans I've ever met. I've known eight-year-olds who could do a better job leading a youth group, and I've known seven-year-olds who were more responsible. Do you really think maturity is optional? Do you think it's cool to be disorganized and…?

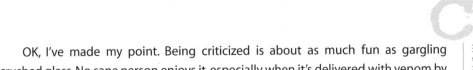

OK, I've made my point. Being criticized is about as much fun as gargling crushed glass. No sane person enjoys it, especially when it's delivered with venom by someone we don't even like to be around. But that doesn't mean we should avoid criticism. In fact, for many reasons we should invite it.

Feedback is the breakfast of champions, and because the work we do matters—and if we want to get better at it—we need all the insight about improving that we can find. We must master the skill of managing criticism.

- **The good, the bad, and the ugly.** We shouldn't become doormats for every cheap shot someone throws our way, however. Criticism comes in three forms: valid, unjustified, and vague. The valid (the good) is the most difficult because it forces us to admit our mistakes. The unjustified (the bad) is often the result of people's unspoken expectations—their fault, not ours. The vague (the ugly) is typically a warning that someone doesn't really like us. The challenge lies in distinguishing between the three and in valuing them appropriately.

- **Expect criticism.** We'll head down the right path if we simply learn to expect criticism. M. Scott Peck opened his international bestseller *The Road Less Traveled* by noting that life is difficult. He went on to state that those of us who accept this fact find that life seems less difficult, but those who avoid the difficulty become neurotic. To which I say "amen" and add this corollary: If you do anything, you will be criticized. If you expect to be criticized, the criticism will hurt less and help more. If you ignore the criticism, you will stagnate and fail.

Think about it. The more people try to do, the more heat they take. As you acquire influence, you acquire critics. Someone out there will take issue with something you've said, done, thought, wore, ate, or saw and will lob rocks at your head. It happened to Christ. It happened to Paul. It has happened to every major religious, political, business, and military leader who has ever lived. Do you really expect to avoid it? Do you want to live a life so inconsequential that you could?

From my observations, there are four key times to expect criticism.

1. When the honeymoon's over. For a few brief moments in time—usually during the first month or so on the job—you're the golden boy or girl. People fawn over you and make favorable comparisons to Billy Graham—"You have such a way with young people," "You have so much energy," "Your work is so important," "We are so lucky to have you." My advice is simple: Enjoy the accolades while they last, but take them for what they are—casual observations from people who desperately want to believe they hired the right person. The honeymoon will not last. You'll know it's over when the first salvo is fired.

2. When you've done something stupid. Let's admit it: We've all done some pretty stupid things in the name of youth ministry. Occasionally we've done such ridiculous things that people have good reason to believe we have single-digit IQs. Shortly after the fund-raiser that loses fourteen hundred dollars or the beefalo banquet that sends eighty-four people to the hospital with food poisoning, you'll take some hits.

3. When everything is going poorly. While Jimmy Carter was president, inflation raced into the stratosphere and Iran took Americans hostage. His fault for either of these events—not to mention a thousand others—is debatable. But they happened on his watch, so he took the licks. Remember, when an elephant is down, even an ant will kick it. Or as one of my predecessors warned me during my first ministry, "They'll love you as long as you're winning."

4. When everything is going well. Human nature being what it is, some people don't want others to do too well. These people appoint themselves "humility sheriffs" and wander around handing out tickets to anyone who is prospering. Pettiness and envy motivate much of this, but some of it has a legitimate basis.

- **It's valid until proven otherwise.** Actually, no matter which quadrant the criticism is coming from, our response should be the same: Assume it is valid. Our first response is generally to begin acting as our own defense attorneys, crafting brilliant responses and impugning the moral character of our critics. But that misses the major point. We *want* criticism. We *want* people to share insights into how we can do better. We *want* people to tell *us*—not others—how we're falling short. It would be nice if the critics' motivation was pure and their delivery was kind, but we should look for the truth in their statements even if not.

- **Count, "One...two...three..."** When you've been attacked, count to ten and recite Proverbs 15:1 before saying anything. The delay will help you avoid escalating the exchange and—if the attack was made publicly—will let someone else come to your defense. (If no one does, the criticism might be something everyone has been thinking.) Besides, people will likely remember the way you respond to your critic as much as they remember what the critic says. So apologize when appropriate, thank the critic for sharing the thoughts, and own your mistakes. Christianity Today attributed Billy Graham's long tenure to his ability to weather conflict; he accepts criticism and apologizes. Likewise, many historians point out that John F. Kennedy survived the Bay of Pigs debacle—a major gaff for the United States—because he took responsibility for the mistake, while Richard Nixon was leveled by charges of a break-in—a minor event in the world scene—because he shifted the blame.

If you start to lose your head, don't be afraid to say so. During a business retreat I was facilitating, an executive director came under sharp attack. Though the criticism's validity was questionable, he accepted it openly. The conversation moved forward until someone lofted a particularly cheap shot. At that point the executive swallowed hard and said, "I need to ask you to restate that. I'm open to criticism, but it must be specific and constructive. I'm feeling attacked right now, and I'm starting to lose my composure. If I do, I'll come out swinging, and this whole process will fall apart." His statement was firm but humble. The attacker apologized and restated his criticism, and the issue was eventually resolved.

• **Request criticism.** One way to avoid big blowouts is to request more frequent feedback. Ask your board or senior pastor for quarterly performance reviews. These people have opinions about the kind of work you're doing and about how you could do better, so you're really just asking for the chance to know their ideas. This formal process may also help you improve early enough to avoid some sniper fire later on.

Delegation

Today's hottest business books spend hundreds of pages saying what the Apostle Paul said in about a dozen words. It's true. Right in the middle of the fourth chapter of Ephesians, Paul spells it out: The job of a pastor is to prepare God's people for ministry.

So we'd have to change a few words for the statement to fit into the business realm. But Paul and many others have made the point: Your job is to get other people to do your job. This concept is called "delegation" by some, "empowerment" by others. Call it what you want. But understand this: It's hard.

In fact, delegating is one of the most unnatural acts known to humanity. But it's not impossible nor uncommon. You can get better—in fact, you must if you want your group to grow much beyond thirty students—but it will take pain and practice.

• **Why pain?** Delegating means letting go of significant projects, not just dirty work. That means two things: (1) You will have to do some of the dirty work yourself, and (2) you will have to take enough risks to lose a little sleep. *What if I give someone a job to do and they fail? What if he forgets to lock up the church? What if she gives a really bad talk? What if…?* You get the picture. If you delegate correctly, you'll certainly have a few worst-case scenarios running through your mind at 2 a.m. I tell most people struggling with delegation that it will take six months of headaches and setbacks. But it's worth it.

• **Why don't we delegate?** Because of a lot of bad reasons. Some people aren't willing to share power. Others are so behind that it would be unfair to delegate. An equal number of people don't delegate because they believe other people can't do as good a job as they can. Which is often true. We usually know our jobs better than the high school kids and volunteers we work with do. But the question is not "Can they do something as well as I can?" The question is "Can someone else do this well enough?"

• **How much should I delegate?** I wouldn't advise you to drop this book, call a student, and shovel onto the student all the responsibility for your upcoming trip to Mexico. Break in people over time. Give them an increasing amount of responsibility with each project. It may help to think about delegation using a fourfold model:

1. *Child*—I'm the parent, and you're the child. I tell you what to do and how to do it. You do it, and then tell me what you did. Responsibility: very little. Reporting: very often.

2. *Apprentice*—I'm the teacher, and you're the learner. There are lots of rules but some flexibility. Responsibility: a bit. Reporting: frequent.

3. *Staff*—I'm the boss, but if all goes well, you'll soon be the boss. I'll let you take

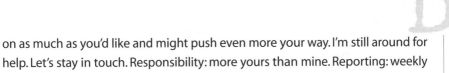

on as much as you'd like and might push even more your way. I'm still around for help. Let's stay in touch. Responsibility: more yours than mine. Reporting: weekly or at your request.

4. Empowered—I'm the chairperson, and you're the president. Go for it. If you want my counsel, you can ask for it. Otherwise, I'll be quiet. You own the project and the worry. Responsibility: total. Reporting: infrequently.

Design your own chart, and create your own ridiculous titles, but be certain that you're clear about what level of delegation is taking place. One senior pastor I worked under would even say, "I'm handing this over to you at a level three (staff)."

• **What should I delegate?** Everything, everything, everything. OK, not everything. You must personally handle a limited number of matters such as some counseling situations and staff hiring and firing. But the overarching rule is "Do all you can to turn as much as you can over to as many people as you can as soon as you can."

Disaster Recovery

At some point in your ministry, you will blow it—I mean really, really blow it. The real question is not "if" or even "when," but "How will you respond when it happens?" I have four suggestions:

1. Take the blame. It's coming your way anyway, so step forward and head off the posse at the pass.

2. Invite criticism. Embrace it. View it as God's chisel. If you earn a reputation as someone who welcomes critical comments, your enemies will be few, and they will likely talk about your faults in front of your face rather than behind your back. (See "Criticism—Receiving" on p. 24.)

3. Look for the upside. If the tree lands on you, you might as well pick the fruit if for no other reason than the tree eventually will be easier to lift.

4. Don't play "holier than thou." The kingdom of God has enough managers. We need leaders—even flawed ones.

E-Mail

We are now waging war on at least four fronts. I'm not talking about the stuff of the *Screwtape Letters* or anything else spiritual, but about the ways we manage information—the daily kind, which used to be limited to phone calls, visitors, and the post office. Now we face an e-mail explosion that won't soon abate. Some claim that the average white-collar worker in the United States is getting more than one hundred e-mail messages a week. Some claim that the number is much higher, and everyone estimates that the number will skyrocket in the coming years.

Actually, I like e-mail. As a person who lives or dies by his network, I find e-mail a great way to interact with lots of people. It beats the phone, which is the ultimate in urgency, and it's easier to manage than voice mail. It's cheaper and faster than the post office, and it's a great leveler of organizations. People I never would have been able to reach by phone have responded to e-mail.

But there are days I can easily spend three or four hours simply sending and receiving e-mail. We clearly need help.

To the Sender

Be brief. Ideally, the reader can see the header and the entire message on one SVGA screen. If you need to send something longer, send it only to those who absolutely must read the whole thing. Send a short summary to others, and offer to send the entire message.

Lay off the colored fonts. I've yet to hit age forty, but I've had to squint to read e-mails that use colorful backgrounds and fonts. Though the first message was novel, I now consider anything in color to be the equivalent of a business letter written in crayon.

Respond quickly. The value of this medium is that it allows quick responses. Don't sit on a message for more than a few days. If you're out of the office and won't be checking your messages, let people know by setting up an automatic reply.

Don't rush your reply. If the issue at hand is dicey, or if you're annoyed, write the message now, but don't send it until tomorrow. When you reread it in the morning, you'll likely find you were too harsh, too emotional, and too wordy—not to mention the fact that you misspelled a few key words and left out half of your main points.

Avoid all caps. IT'S THE WRITTEN EQUIVALENT OF SHOUTING.

Avoid emoticons. Sorry, but not everyone finds emotional icons (emoticons) cute. : (

Tell the story in the subject line. Generic headings such as "meeting agenda" or "follow up" aren't much better than leaving the header box blank. Take fifteen seconds to precisely describe your message so it'll be clear to the receivers, too.

Be considerate. Don't copy long messages. If you must forward a message to someone else, send only the relevant parts. And if you really, really, really must forward a tenth-generation message, trim the sixty-two miles of headers and get rid of all of the ">" signs.

Be careful. Church e-mail is probably not the place to send or receive jokes and other personal matters. Assume that whatever you write can end up in the hands of the court or, worse yet, the church board. Once created, most e-mail systems save even deleted messages. Be careful about what you say and promise.

Be smart. Bill Gates isn't offering people one thousand dollars, Disney isn't giving away free vacations, and Neiman Marcus doesn't have a two-hundred-dollar cookie recipe. There is no kidney theft ring in New Orleans, and no plutonium showers blanket the eastern seaboard. NASA hasn't found a lost day, and Craig Sherold from England isn't dying of cancer and doesn't want your business card. If you get a message that sounds too good to be true or too bizarre to be believable, it probably is— even if someone fourteen generations back says, "I checked this out, and it's legit."

Write important notes by hand. In a world of e-mail, a handwritten note will stand out.

To the Receiver

Filter the spam. By some estimates, as much as 15 percent of all e-mail messages, 30 percent for America Online users, is spam (unsolicited, unwanted, electronic junk mail). What can you do?

- Place a filter on your e-mail.
- Use two mailboxes—one for private correspondence with friends, family, and work, and the other for more public discourse such as chat rooms.
- Never cruise the Web, where spam "robots" cruise to collect private e-mail addresses.
- Never respond to the line "If you want to be removed from this list, send e-mail to…" Your request may actually place you on a spam list.

Use one touch. You should open your "snail mail" over the recycle bin, ready to discard what you can, respond to what you can't, and file what you must. You should open your e-mail the same way. The goal is to touch the document as few times as possible, and your options are simple: Delete it, respond to it, or file it.

Follow the FIFO rule. If you scan the in-box to choose what you want to read, you'll be left with a long list of awful messages at the end of the day. Thus the First In First Out (FIFO) rule.

Files

There are two major types of files: action and standing. Action files are standing files you need often. Most people have about ten, including things to copy, things to read, things to file, and things to talk to the boss or assistant about. The standing files can generally be divided along three lines: administration, Bible study, and everything else.

You'll be able to file with the best of them if you follow these four simple rules:

1. Don't file it. There are undoubtedly millions of file drawers in this country collectively holding billions of pieces of paper. According to those who have nothing better to do than study these things, about 80 percent of those files will never be looked at again (Barbara Hemphill, *Taming the Paper Tiger).* When in doubt, throw it out. Most of us make the mistake of looking at a piece of paper and asking, "Can I imagine a scenario in which I might need this piece of paper?" And of course unless it's tissue paper you just used to wipe your nose, the answer is yes. The question we should ask is "If I need this piece of paper in the future and don't have it, how much trouble will I be in?" If the answer is "I'll get fined, fired, or put into prison," then file it. But if all you have to do is walk down the hall and pull a copy out of someone else's files, then deep-six it. Generally speaking, you don't want to keep anything someone else is keeping. The more stuff you file, the more difficult it is to find what you need.

Place the papers you're not quite willing to part with in a box, and label it with a throwaway date. Put the box in the church basement or some other storage facility, and forget about it. If you need something, you can find it. When you stumble into the church basement years later and trip over the box, throw it away. (Do not—I repeat, do not—open it and start looking through it.)

2. Design a system that works for you. Those who do the filing get to design their own system. They should make it as simple as possible and keep a list of all the files. If you do this, you can recruit volunteers who don't have a degree in library science to help you file.

3. File, don't pile. Most people have more than thirty-six hours of work sitting on their desks, which is not as much of a surprise as it is a problem. Case in point: While working on your Bible study, you glance at a stack of papers in the corner. The sheet on top is an important letter you had forgotten about. You pick up the letter, wince, and then look for a better place to set it—a place where you won't forget it. But when you refocus a couple of minutes later, your eyes wander again. By moving the first letter, you uncovered another important letter. (Remember, everything on your desk is there because it is important.) You can do this all day and never actually do any work. So if you save something, get it off your desk and into a file.

4. File it where you'll find it. The trick is to think big, not small. When you look for a spot to keep the receipts for next month's financial report, you're better off placing them in a general file containing all your administrative duties for next month than you are placing them in a folder just for receipts. If you start a whole new file, you'll not only end up with millions of file folders, but you'll also spend an eternity trying to remember what you called it—is it under F for "financial report" or M for "money" or R for "receipts" or T for "treasurer"?

Fiscal Control

Many years ago during the middle of the Jim and Tammy Bakker debacle, a few church leaders pulled me aside and asked how I handled the college group's money. When I explained that I stuffed the offering in my pocket and took it home for my wife to count and deposit, they rolled their eyes. When they found out I was handling almost as much money as the church itself, they about croaked. To be honest, once I started explaining things, I wasn't feeling too good about it myself. The system had worked, but there were a dozen ways for it to fail; if it had, my reputation would have gone south along with the system. From that point on, we introduced a much tighter system of financial control.

• **Two are better than one.** Whenever you collect money, have two people

Suddenly the youth group's budget problems made sense.

"What do you mean we're out of money? We still have checks."

count it, record the amount on a slip of paper, and initial it. That record, along with the money, should then immediately be put into a drop box or safe.

• **Limit check-signing authority.** Few banks will still agree to check for double signatures, but it's not a bad idea to set up that control internally for amounts over several hundred dollars. Also, anyone who opens the mail and consequently may come across contribution checks should not have check-signing powers.

• **Restrict spending authority.** One of the perennial problems youth pastors face is other people draining their budget. The senior pastor deducts $250 for the confirmation class books he ordered. Someone's mom, certain that your office needs curtains, makes them and then submits her expenses to the church treasurer along with a note that says, "Deduct from the youth budget." I was so frequently surprised by our bill from the copy center—people I didn't even know were signing for youth ministry copies—that I closed the account. Establish and limit who can spend youth ministry money.

• **Establish petty cash restrictions.** It can be a real pain to find someone who can cut and sign a check so that you can pick up a few office supplies, so having a petty cash drawer makes sense. But there are so many problems with petty cash that you have to be absolutely certain the amounts remain true to their name—petty. For the record, my experience with petty cash is that it will be stolen at least once every eighteen months. So hide it, lock it, and keep the balance low.

• **Receipt all gifts and payments.** Always leave a paper trail for any church money you spend or receive. Refuse to allow parents to hand you ten dollars for their child's retreat deposit as you walk across the fellowship hall. They need a receipt, and you need a record. Otherwise you will end up with thirty-five dollars in your pocket and no clue how it got there. Do not pay a speaker out of retreat cash. Pay with a check so you have a record. Run everything through the books. Also provide tax receipts for donations. Gifts in kind should be acknowledged in writing, but don't get caught up in declaring a value for the item. Let the giver do that.

• **Do not touch the money.** Another way to advertise your integrity is to stop touching the money at all. After I was questioned about the offering, I had other people collect everything—retreat deposits, petty cash, mission funds, and car wash proceeds. This not only helped me avoid any impressions of impropriety, but it also helped me avoid any impressions of greed. After all, few images are worse than a youth pastor with his hands filled with wads of youth group money.

• **Rely on your sense of smell.** Finally, do not be afraid to trust your gut. When it comes to money, if something doesn't look right, it probably isn't. Rely on common sense. If last year's car wash brought in $325 and this year's car wash was even bigger but netted less money, something is wrong. When things smell bad, dig around until you find out why.

• **Become embezzlement-proof.** Who would embezzle money from the youth group? You, for starters. "Taking the first dollar is the hardest," notes Chris Renzelman, a veteran youth pastor and the Northwest Director for the National Network. "After the first dollar, it is all a matter of zeros. Do you take ten? one hundred? more? The decision to take money has already been made." And few people would have an easier time taking money than a youth leader, which makes the need for control that much greater. We need fiscal control to protect ourselves from temptation, and we need fiscal control to advertise to others—especially our students—that we keep tight books. "If you are very conscientious in how you deal with money and you always give people a receipt for deposits, then in the event of a problem, you are far more likely to receive the benefit of the doubt," says Renzelman.

Free Time

If you're reading this book to find more free time, let me be very clear. There are only three ways you will ever get more time:

1. Do what you currently do more quickly.
2. Delegate what you've done in the past to someone else.
3. Stop doing some of the things you currently do.

Of these three ways, the real gains come with the last one.

Friends

About eighteen months into my first ministry, my wife looked across the dinner table and asked me, "Do you know what your problem is?"

Since I didn't have any idea what she was talking about and I couldn't narrow the list of eighty possible answers down to one or two, the question hung ominously in the air for about sixty seconds. Finally, swallowing hard, I looked across the table and said, "No."

"Your problem," she said, "is that you don't have any friends. But even worse is that you don't even know it. You've got lots and lots of acquaintances and they all think you're just great, but you don't have any real friends. You're hanging out with college students all day long. It's sad."

Ouch!

I protested, but of course in the end she won because she was right. Way too many people in ministry have no friends. And way too many of those people don't even know it.

So what are friends? Without getting esoteric here, let me simply tell you what they are not.

- **They're not people who ask you to pray over a meal.** "Aren't we fortunate tonight to have Mike and his family over for dinner? Since we have a pastor in the house, let's ask him to pray." If someone views you as a professional Christian or a spiritual superior, then he or she has an idol and you have a groupie.

- **They're not on your staff.** It's great to be friends with the people you work with, but if you can't name someone outside of the staff team who's a close buddy, then you're a working drone, not a human being. If no one on the staff team can name someone outside of the staff that he or she spends great and consistent downtime with, then your ministry team is dangerously enmeshed.

- **They're not your students.** Enough said.

- **They're not people who would get rattled if you said you were struggling spiritually.** You need people around you whose walk with Christ is independent of yours. If their faith would suffer because you share some of your doubts, then you're always on call. You're their pastor, not their friend.

- **I'm tempted to write that they're not people who go to your church.** But instead I'll say this: They're not people who care what job you have. Friends are friends. If they'd be less interested in spending time with you if you exchanged youth ministry for a teaching position, then you have some macabre type of performance relationship, not a friendship.

I could go on, but you get the point. Life is short. You need friends. They take time, so work them into your schedule.

The Future

As a rule, youth ministers react. We seldom spend time seriously thinking about tomorrow's issues—in part because we seldom spend time seriously thinking—preferring instead to respond to today's needs.

While that isn't all bad, since we have real people with immediate problems who look to us for help right now, it's not all good either. Leaders must see past the horizon if they're ever to make a substantial difference. To dedicate some time to this, here are several tools to master:

- **Trend projections.** Way back in junior high, you were given graph paper and taught how to plot points on the "x" and "y" axes. Your finished product, complete with the big hole where you erased through the paper, showed some type of correlation. For instance, by plotting bunnies on one axis and time on the other, you determined that two bunnies plus nine months equals about seven hundred thousand bunnies. (Trends like that are easy to spot.) Well, today's computers can plot more points on more axes than our alphabet has letters—without making holes. If you show these charts to your church leaders, they'll start to think you're pretty smart. If you show them to a denomination exec, you'll be dubbed a futurist and invited to speak at your next national conference.

An example: To find out where your church will be in ten years, study your congregation. Add ten years to everyone who is coming today, and ask yourself who will be in your congregation then. (It's seldom a pretty sight.) Our church did this several years ago and discovered that no one would be around to turn out the lights. This shouldn't have come as a surprise, considering we were doing about twenty funerals for every wedding, but it was surprising nonetheless.

The downside: When employment specialists tried to project job openings for generation Xers, they didn't predict how many would forgo corporate America for entrepreneurial ventures. When the United Nations used trend projections to plot population figures for Africa, they didn't count on an AIDS epidemic decimating countries. In other words, our assumptions matter, and trends change.

• **Issue analysis.** Given enough time, enough guns, and enough pickup trucks, those who shoot traffic signs for sport will eventually create the world's great literary works in Braille. Given even more time than that, you'd be able to keep on top of the issues affecting the future. However, since you have little free time, you'll be forced to choose fewer issues. This is the logic behind issue analysis. You choose a handful of critical issues, and watch them closely.

An example: Developers can ignore the teen birthrate, the number of body parts pierced on today's adolescents, and the rise of postmodern thought among high school kids in order to focus on wetland permits, the price of timber, and the general economy. You should do the opposite: focus on those issues that affect adolescents.

The downside: You watch the wrong issue, and you learn the wrong stuff. You ignore the right issue, and you get mowed down.

• **Delphi polling.** A recent survey suggests that any survey suggesting things we don't agree with is dismissed as a stupid survey. But my own survey, taken right now (sample size: one thirty-eight-year-old male, very informed, and grossly undercompensated), suggests that Delphi polling is different. With Delphi polling, you forget about uninformed masses and go straight to the pundits (those folks who blab on Sunday morning talk shows when they should be in church).

An example: If you wanted to use Delphi polling to predict the teen pregnancy rate in the year 2015, you would gather one hundred of the leading youth culture experts and ask their opinions. Then you'd write up the results, and send them back to the experts for a second round. You'd ask those who had extreme views to clarify their thinking. You'd ask the others to read everyone else's guesses and then vote again. You'd repeat the process until some consensus was reached.

The downside: The Delphi process tends to act like a bad mattress—everyone meets in the middle. Also, a panel of one hundred experts in the field may completely miss developments outside their field; the railroad engineer predicts faster trains, not airplanes.

• **Intuitive insights.** Those of us who survived college learned to treat essay tests as a true art form, restating the few facts provided with such flare and panache that we got at least half credit. But a select few of us discovered that we were especially good at the multiple-choice questions. Most of these people moved to Reno, honed their skill at blackjack, and retired before they turned twenty-five. But some—John Nasbit, Faith Popcorn, and their ilk—became futurists. Their lives consist of reading a few articles, staring at the wall for about three minutes, and then making some really good guesses. Occasionally they will say things like "mom-food" or "cocooning," for which they will be paid about $250,000.

The upside: Often they are right.

The downside: Often they are wrong.

• **Prophetic insights.** Sometimes God shares special insights with people, who are instructed to give voice to these matters and call the church back to task.

Examples: Isaiah, Jeremiah, and Jonah come to mind.

The upside: Who better to brief us on the future than the One who holds it in his hands?

The downside: People—even those with the best of intentions—often confuse the odd feeling caused by eating too much at lunch with a message from God. They announce—typically with such modest introductions as "God told me" or "I have a word of knowledge"—things about the future that just aren't so. (Most involve the need to send them large sums of money.) The Old Testament is pretty clear that the biblical folks were graded on a strict curve; 100 percent earned an A, and 99 percent earned the death penalty. But today these folks are free to be wrong again and again and again.

• **The consequence tree.** The official scientific term for this important and delicate tool is the "then what exercise." Here's how it works: You get a handful of reasonably bright people in the room (OK, if you don't know anybody like that, go ahead and use your friends), read someone's educated guess about a particular aspect of the future—virtual reality, for example—and ask, "Then what?" For example, "If we could put funky little glasses on folks who assaulted their senses in ways Walt Disney could only dream of, what would happen?"

"Well, Disney stock would tumble, the pornographers would elevate their craft to even more wicked levels, and kids enamored with virtual reality would start to find youth group pretty boring."

After round one, you do it all over again, but this time you ask what the consequences of the consequences are. For example, "What would happen if virtual reality meant kids were bored by the way we do things today?"

The upside: You get some extra time to think about some very important issues.

• **Contextual forecasting**. In an effort to take over the world, many organizations will perform trend analyses on a variety of topics such as the economy, technology, politics, culture, the hemline on skirts, and the temperature of the Pacific. They will use this information to try to figure out what their competition is thinking—which assumes that their competition actually is thinking—and may even make some estimates on how likely all of these things are to happen. The goal, once again, is to figure out tomorrow's challenges today.

The upside: Unless you are a really dim bulb and really mess up the trend projections phase of this exercise, you learn a lot.

• **Scenario forecasting.** The last game in a futurist's toy box is scenario forecasting, for which futurists use the upside of all the tricks and tools listed above to make some guesses about the future. Then they create three possible scenarios to describe it. One is optimistic: Bill Gates leaves you all of his stock options. One is likely: Your world is more complex, and you have less free time and a lot less hair. And one is pessimistic: Your treasurer skips town with the cash, the church rents itself out as a bingo hall, and you have even less free time than before and absolutely no hair. The futurists think about how to respond to each scenario.

An example: In the *Art of the Longview,* Peter Schwartz describes how he created a scenario for Shell Oil that included the fall of the Soviet Union. When it actually happened, Schwartz had the joy of trumping the CIA in their own game, and Shell moved quickly to secure a large market share in Eastern Europe.

(For more information, see the books of Tom Sine, Christian futurist.)

Goal Setting

If it's true that only a fine line separates vision and hallucination, then the question becomes "How do we establish wise and God-honoring goals without slipping over the edge?" I think the answer lies in the following questions:

- **How long do you plan to stay where you are?** If you plan to move to a different church every few years, your vision obviously will be limited by your time frame. Generally, we tend to overestimate what we can do in one year and underestimate what we can do in five. My personal experience is that the longer I stay in one place, the more effective I become and the larger my vision grows.

- **What kind of experience have you had?** Many young leaders bring excellent vision and truckloads of energy but not quite enough skill to pull things off on the scale they hope for. The younger you are, the more important it is to have other visionaries around you to help keep you in line. Too much vision may do more harm than good.

- **How big is your area?** I was once asked to speak at a high school retreat in Nebraska. When I asked how many kids they expected to show up, the youth pastor laughed and said, "Well, there are probably more kids in your church than in my state." Obviously, the size of his youth group is necessarily affected by the number of teenagers in his state. Building a thousand-member group should probably not be his vision.

Groupthink

Though most of us can do some pretty lame things all by ourselves, we can really mess things up if we have help. For world-class stupid ideas, you almost always need a committee. Just take four or five like-minded folks, and place them in an atmosphere that values getting along more highly than it values getting things done. Then, as the leader, be sure to voice your opinion early, often, and loudly. Make sure everyone knows that challenging faulty thinking will earn him or her the "critical spirit" label. With a few other factors, you're almost guaranteed to cook up plans so risky and naive that no individual member of the group would ever even think of recommending them on his or her own. It's called "groupthink."

Groupthink can be fostered by leaders who don't tolerate dissent or by leaders who offer their people so much encouragement that everyone begins to underestimate potential problems. Groupthink usually pops up quickly, feeds on the group's energy, then wreaks havoc before anyone realizes what's going on. For example, Sheri thinks a month-long junior high lock-in sounds even more stupid than the indoor bonfire idea you tried last fall, but she keeps her thoughts to herself because she doesn't want to cause problems. David and Fred misread Sheri's silence for support and decide not to voice their own concerns. Soon the idea is adopted even though you're the only one who thinks it sounds like fun.

The more complex an issue is, the more likely it is that groupthink will take over, because people are less likely to disagree when they don't understand all the factors. Groupthink is also a high risk when membership in the group is valued, because people don't want to risk whining their way off the team. How to stop it?

• **Reward critical thinking.** Go out of your way to invite thoughtful criticism of new proposals—especially your own. You might find it wise to appoint a "devil's advocate" to attack an idea. If one person is given a chance to point out weaknesses, others are more likely to do so.

• **Do not mistake silence for consent.** Risk-takers tend to dominate meetings, so don't assume that quiet or silent people are in agreement.

• **Form groups to critique new ideas.** People who hesitate to speak in a large-group setting might be more comfortable with fewer people.

• **Don't state your opinion too early.** Volunteers, especially those new to your team, will seldom criticize what you've endorsed. If you've already decided to act on a new idea, it's a waste of time to hold a meeting about the issue.

• **Give people time to think through major proposals.** After the initial enthusiasm wears off, people are more likely to spot problems and weaknesses.

"Now I want this to be a team decision. So Jeff,
you say something in favor of it first."

- **Seek wide exposure for new steps.** Consider bringing in an outside "expert" to review your plans. At the very least, talk to people you suspect will be against the idea. If you can't convince them of the plan's merits, maybe it's because the plan doesn't have any.

- **Run a pilot program.** If the idea has survived the first six steps, consider running a test before you allocate major funds.

(Based on Mike Woodruff's article "How to Win the Game of Hiring," Youthworker Journal, Fall 1993.)

In a growing ministry, you are what you hire. The talents and gifts—as well as the theological convictions, lifestyles, personalities, and family lives—of the people who fill the leadership slots make or break your overall efforts to reach the students. And your first two hires—the ones you typically make before you have any experience hiring staff—are the two most important ones because they represent 50 and 33 percent of your workforce.

So unless you enjoy bad headaches and losing about forty thousand dollars, which is the average cost of a bad church hire, you'll read over this section about twenty-three times.

• **Start with good help.** Robert Dingman, a search consultant who has helped many church and parachurch organizations select staff, notes, "When the search committee is formed, half the damage is already done." Your staff might make an ideal selection committee, but they may not. Consider augmenting them with your senior pastor or board or possibly members of the congregation. If this is a really critical hire, consider bringing in a consultant—possibly a youth minister from a local church—to offer an objective third-party voice. At the same time the selection team is

"I'm a little concerned about this line that reads,
'And other items too numerous to mention.' "

formed, launch a prayer team. Their responsibility is obvious.

- **Think first.** The next step is to write both a job description and a personal profile. The job description answers questions such as "What will this person be responsible for?" "Who will the person report to?" and "How much will the salary be?" A personal profile paints a picture of the kind of person and the skills and passions you're interested in. Rework the description and profile until you've got it right. Weight the skills according to their importance, which will keep you from being overly impressed by high-powered people who could do a great job, but not the job you're hiring for. The typical mistake is to rush the hiring process, which means you'll get to do it again six months and forty thousand dollars from now.

- **Look in your own backyard.** It's almost always best to promote from within. These people have built-in advantages—they like you, they understand your vision, and they're already part of your group's culture. Outsiders will need at least a year—assuming you hire the right outsider—to learn what a church member already knows. The candidacy process is like a courtship dance; everyone's on his or her best behavior. And even if you use all the tricks and tools available to help you understand someone, nothing can replace the test of time.

- **Network.** If you need to go outside your ministry to fill a position, use your network. Contact friends or churches with cutting-edge programs, and describe the kind of person you need. Ask for names and leads. Chances are that the type of person you want is currently successfully engaged in ministry somewhere else and may not be thinking about leaving until you make contact.

You might also consider contacting seminary placement offices, but keep your eyes open. You're signing on to help complete the graduate's training. And realize that it's more expensive to keep hiring, training, and losing recent seminary graduates than it is to just offer a larger salary to someone with a proven track record.

- **Make the offer.** The final decision is often quite easy. One candidate emerges. You select the candidate, and hopefully he or she accepts you. (But don't be too quick to throw away the files for your other top applicants.) Usually the official offer is made in writing and includes details such as starting date, details of compensation, vacation days, and a clear duration of the offer.

- **Don't leave people hanging.** After someone has accepted a position, you should quickly contact the other applicants and let them know the outcome.

- **Here are three more hiring tips.**

  1. Be prepared for the process to take a while. In business the rule of thumb is that for every ten thousand dollars you're offering in salary, you should expect one month for the search. You're better off hiring temporary help or holding back expansion plans than you are rushing this process.

2. Never hire someone you can't fire. I once hired my assistant's girlfriend and got away with it, but I doubt I'll do it again. This is why some churches will not hire church members for staff positions. It's also why you shouldn't hire the senior pastor's son.

3. Don't ignore the candidate's spouse. If possible, fly out the candidate's spouse for the interview. This person shouldn't sit in on the first interview, but the spouse can't be ignored.

Hold-Harmless Agreements

Hold-harmless forms are contracts whereby one party agrees to waive any liability for negligence on the part of another party for injuries or damages related to certain events. They will not always prevent you from being sued, but they are a good idea, especially if written correctly.

• **Be specific.** Spell out which rights are being waived. A hold-harmless agreement with broad, sweeping language that protects someone from all liability, or one that is ambiguous or unclear, is likely to be invalid.

• **Be clear.** Avoid "legalese" as much as possible. The form's intention must be clear to the causal reader.

• **Capitalize.** CAPITALIZE or **boldface** key sections to draw attention to them. Have the signer initial certain sections to indicate that he or she has read and understood them.

• **Make sure that parents or guardians sign.** Hold-harmless agreements are compromised if the signer is under the age of majority (eighteen in most states). Have students age eighteen or older list their age on the documents.

• **Get legal advice.** Even if you do everything right, waivers do have exceptions, which are governed by statutory or case laws. Develop a working relationship with an attorney in your church, and seek his or her counsel when crafting a waiver.

Insurance

Bad things happen, so are you properly insured? There are five relevant types of insurance for your church to consider.

1. Accident/medical. Most students in your group have medical coverage through their parents; however, short-term primary policies ("primary" is the insurance that pays first, before any standard coverage) are available for special events. If you purchase this type of coverage, be sure you understand the restrictions. Some policies do not apply outside of the country. Others cover accidents but not illnesses. In general, you should be prepared to pay cash for medical care any time you leave the country, you should be certain everyone has insurance, and you should have a record of everyone's carrier any time you take an extended trip.

2. Automobile. Whenever you're driving students, make certain that the vehicle is insured. One youth minister was in an accident that left a young woman in a permanent vegetative state. The parents sued and were awarded a one-million-dollar settlement. Had the church not taken out a supplemental auto-protection policy covering the youth pastor, the church would have lost its building and the youth pastor would have lost his house. At the very least…

- Churches need secondary auto coverage, a plan that kicks in after the driver's individual coverage has been exhausted.
- Drivers need liability coverage, which secondary policies often do not include.
- You need to read the policies and note the restrictions. Most policies don't cover drivers younger than twenty-five and don't cover vehicles driven outside of the country.

3. Church liability. Liability coverage protects you in the event of a lawsuit resulting from any work you have done as a pastor. To minimize your liability, always inform parents of risks and ask them to sign hold-harmless agreements (see p. 45). Also check with your insurance agent to be sure the church's liability insurance extends to you. After years of being assured by a church that I was covered, I finally spoke with our agent. I was told that because my name had never been added to the policy, I was not insured. If you work part time or aren't ordained, you're at even greater risk of being left off the church's overall plan. Note: Liability coverage seldom applies outside of the country. Few churches have the special rider. If you decide you can't afford a policy that's international in scope, be certain you have an excellent accident/medical plan.

4. Pastoral liability. This coverage is usually a professional-policy endorsement on the church's overall plan. It covers you as a counselor and is relatively inexpensive.

5. Personal property. This coverage may not be worth its cost. Most church property or content policies are secondary in nature, meaning your homeowners or renters insurance is expected to kick in first. Also, these policies usually have such high deductibles—some as high as five thousand dollars—that it's a lot simpler to just lock your door.

Though it will be less enjoyable than a migraine headache, you or someone you trust should read all the insurance documents. Also ask to be invited to the church's yearly insurance review so you can ask questions. If you find that the church doesn't routinely review its policies, ask the board to make that a priority. The proper time to sort through the complexities of proper insurance coverage is now, not two days after your next crisis.

Interruptions

The typical business person averages ten minutes between interruptions, making them the number one management headache in the world. Our job is subject to as many interruptions—or more. What to do?

• **Realize that not every interruption is an interruption.** You're both paid and called to focus on others. Some of what may strike you as inconvenient is really a divine appointment.

• **Realize that most interruptions are your fault.** When you design a program that revolves around you, don't be surprised when everything revolves around you.

• **Give people the information they need before they interrupt you.** Think ahead about questions you're likely to be asked, then post the answers on your Web site, include them in the church newsletter, or set up a phone hot line so people can retrieve what they need without pestering you.

• **Set up office hours.** Professors do. If people want you, then steer them toward times that make sense. Better yet, hang out at the school when students are getting out of class. In thirty minutes, you can reach lots of students and head off lots of interruptions.

• **Evaluate your interruptions.** Keep a log of your interruptions for two weeks. If you see, as I suspect you will, that 80 percent of your interruptions are caused by about four people, then you can take them aside and say, "I'm really trying to protect my study time. Could you help me out by not interrupting me between 9 a.m. and lunch?"

Interviewing Prospective Staff

Interviews typically don't provide the kinds of information people need to make a wise selection. They're usually unstructured and too short. Often within fifteen minutes of the time the person walks through the door, everyone in the room has a gut feeling that—right or wrong—they will stick with. Nevertheless, people want to see candidates interact with others and want to get a glimpse into their personalities. An interview does that. If you've narrowed the field to two or three candidates, it's time to fly them out and conduct interviews.

Situational interviews—interviews in which you ask the candidate, "What would you do in the following situation?"—can be helpful because what people say they'll do and what they'll actually do are pretty close. Be sure to take notes, especially if you're interviewing a number of people, and ask each candidate the same questions. The latter not only protects you against charges of bias, but also helps you evenly compare candidates.

If possible, fly candidates out for close to a week, and have them stay at your home. This gives you a better chance to get to know them. Right out of seminary, I stayed for a week with a pastor in Orlando while interviewing with a church. After the first couple of days, we loved each other; after a few more days, my wife picked up on some significant issues that would affect my job. The extended stay helped us get over our infatuation with the position.

You can find entire books containing nothing but penetrating interview questions. Unfortunately, the same authors write second books telling job applicants how to answer those same questions, so the only winner is the author who sells the books.

While the following questions are not meant to be all-inclusive—in fact, I'm leaving it to you to ask the obvious questions like "Tell me how you came to Christ" and "Describe your philosophy of ministry"—they may pique your thinking.

- **Question**: When you think of a big youth group, what number jumps into your head?

    Reason: If a candidate says fifty is big, don't expect his or her ministry to grow much larger than that.

- **Question**: Describe three setbacks and how you overcame them.

    Reason: Peak performers learn from setbacks and go on. Insecure people try to hide their previous mistakes.

- **Question**: Why are you leaving your current position?

    Reason: You want to beware of people who bad-mouth other people or other churches. It goes without saying that if you hire them, they will one day bad-mouth you.

- **Question**: What did you like most about your last job, and why?

    Reason: Listen to why they liked what they did. This will help you understand if they really enjoy a challenge.

- **Question**: Describe emergencies in the past for which you've had to reschedule your time.

Reason: This is a more effective way of asking, "Are you willing to work extra hours if necessary?"

- **Question**: What questions do you have of us?

  Reason: Beware of any candidate who doesn't try to learn as much as possible about the youth group he or she will be serving. These candidates are either overly anxious, naive, or uninterested.

- **Question**: Are there aspects of youth ministry you don't enjoy?

  Reason: Asking, "What do you like to do?" is not a reliable guide to what a candidate does well—for example, I would like to be a NFL quarterback, but I'd do a poor job. But what we don't like to do correlates highly with what we do poorly.

Don't spend much time on theological questions because they can take forever. Instead, send candidates a copy of your statement of faith, and then ask if they would be comfortable signing it.

Interviewing Your Prospective Boss

Interviews go both ways. They grill you, and you grill them back. Yet typically, youth ministers are so excited about a new position—*Someone is going to pay me to*

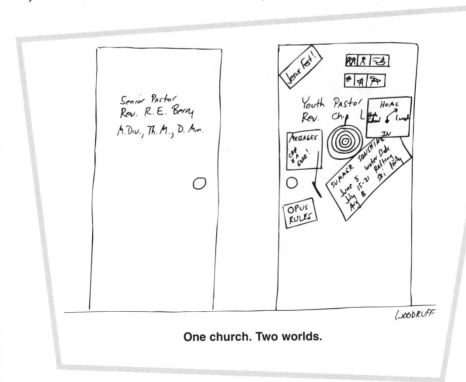

One church. Two worlds.

hang out with kids!—that we don't ask questions. Expectations are left unstated, and that almost guarantees rough water ahead. Next time, don't just ask about the size of the youth group, the amount of the paycheck, and the availability of the church gym. Evaluate the senior pastor. Here are five things to look for:

1. How long did the previous youth pastor stay? If you're the third high school director hired in as many months, I wouldn't sign a long lease. Those people left for a reason. Conversely, a church with a pastor whose staff members all have long tenures, or a church in which even those who leave the staff have great things to say about the senior pastor, has a lot going for it. Ask why the previous youth pastor left and if it would it be possible to talk with him or her.

2. Do you have any youth ministry experience? It's not critical that your senior pastor has survived a dozen lock-ins and sumo wrestling marathons, but I think those who have usually make better allies. In addition to understanding the stresses you face and the headaches senior pastors can cause, they will also be better able to coach you because they understand your world.

3. Can I learn from this person? Much to everyone's dismay, we end up spending more time with people we work with than the person we marry. You can't help but be shaped by your colleagues, especially your boss. During the interview as you look across the desk at the senior pastor, ask yourself, "If I end up thinking and acting like this person, would that be a good thing? Does he or she have some important qualities or skills I could learn from?" If the answer is no, then seriously rethink any decision to accept the position.

4. Do we differ enough to make this work? If you and your boss could pass as clones, then one of you isn't really necessary. (Try to guess which one will be asked to leave.) You do want a common vision and enough similar interests to be compatible, but you also want enough differences to make the team work.

5. Will I be expected to do youth ministry or to direct it? There is a big difference between the two. You want to be on staff at a church that has hired you to help them reach kids. You do not want to get trapped by the expectation that you'll do it all by yourself.

Leading Meetings When You're Not In Charge

There's a real trick to improving meetings someone else is leading. Here are some suggestions.

• **Don't attend.** Don't play hooky—it's poor form—but do resign from meetings that don't deliver enough bang for the buck. Because the session meetings at our church used to drag on through several presidential administrations, I asked to be excused for all but the most important ones. No one objected. Once the meetings became streamlined, I still stayed away. Why attend any meeting I don't need to?

• **If meetings wander, keep minutes.** The last thing you want to do is volunteer for more work; however, if a meeting leader is unable to force closure or follow through—meaning you're forever talking about the same issues—you can actually take charge simply by keeping minutes. When the meeting starts to drift off the subject, step in and say, "I'm sorry, but we changed subjects, and it's unclear to me what was resolved about the last issue" or "I'm confused. We decided to take this action, but I didn't catch who was in charge or when that person will report back to this committee." If people give you dirty looks—and a few will—look at them innocently and say, "It's for the minutes. I'm just trying to get all of this information down for the minutes."

At a particularly long staff meeting, Youth Pastor Billy McGee made history by asking for a ten-minute work break.

L

- **No agenda? Make one up yourself.** If the meeting chair is habitually starting meetings with, "Well, what should we talk about today?" or distributing agendas as meetings begin, offer to help. "I know you're really busy, but it sure would help me to receive an agenda a few days before the meeting. How about if I prepare one early in the week and run it by you for modifications? If you need to add something, great. If not, I'll distribute it two days early." Needless to say, if you control the agenda, you control the meeting.

- **Volunteer to chair a subcommittee.** When too many people start debating an issue or when people begin to repeat themselves, do everyone a favor and volunteer to lead a small task force to study the issue and take action. Two hours into one marathon session, I volunteered to chair a subcommittee to deal with the selection of mission candidates. Everyone was so sick of the discussion that they not only agreed to my proposal, but also agreed to my plea that the subcommittee's recommendations be viewed as binding. (I didn't want another debate at the next meeting.) I chose my team on the spot, and we made the decisions during a five-minute break twenty minutes later. It's seldom that simple, but you usually can get a lot more done with fewer people.

- **Learn Robert's Rules of Order.** I know. You would rather eat sand than study this stuff, but in large meetings it really can help. Besides, sooner or later contentious debates need rules, and Robert's Rules of Order are the most universally recognized. Note: By learning about 20 percent of the rules, you will know enough to guide 80 percent of the situations. You'll also know enough to shut down the meeting bullies who want to ramrod their own agendas through. Remember, preparation makes up for lack of talent.

Learning

A while back, my six-year-old son was doing what six-year-olds do best—complaining about school—when he hit on a brilliant idea. "Dad," he said, his voice buoyant with optimism, "if I have to keep going to school because people want me to learn *something,* then why don't you just tell me what that *something* is? Then I'll know it and can stay home from school and play."

Oh, to be six again. Oh, to believe that the body of knowledge we're suppose to acquire is small enough and static enough to master. Of course it's not. With scientists expanding our information base at an exponential rate and with technology inventing and reinventing itself at a dizzying pace, we fall further behind by the nanosecond. Not to mention the ever-expanding libraries of information we're expected to sort through to keep our union card in youth ministry: missions, evangelism, youth culture, church growth, postmodernity, counseling, small groups, and—oh, yeah—the Bible.

We have no choice but to learn. Every month, every week, every day, constantly, it's learn or die.

Which means we must create a culture of learning, an environment in which our students and staff grow wise instead of simply processing information. It's a steep hill and a lifelong task without shortcuts. But the more I learn about learning and the more I observe those who seem to be doing it well, the more I am convinced that it can be done.

• **Make use of learning styles.** Some people learn by watching, others by reading, some by listening, and most by doing; be ready to adapt your approach to the target audience. High school teachers rely too heavily on formal presentations, and youth workers rely too heavily on events. Find a balance that works.

• **Make learners teach.** Ever fall asleep during a message? Ever fall asleep during one you were giving? I'm amazed at how little I knew about the Old Testament until I started to teach my way through it. You might be better versed in Levitical legislation than I am, but the principle holds. People remember what they themselves say, not what you say. So get them to say it. This applies both to the Gospel of John and to the safety rules for using the church van.

• **Invest in your people and in yourself.** The American Society for Training and Development estimates that "true learning organizations will spend between 3 percent and 6 percent of their payrolls on training." With our success measured in souls instead of market share, surely we're spending more. Right?

Hardly. How much have you invested in your staff? How many classes, seminars, or conferences have you sent them to? Look at last year's budget to see. And while you're there, see how much you spent on yourself.

• **Learn something every week.** If you were blessed with a quick mind and decent people skills, you can bluff your way through the first ten years of ministry. But if you want to finish strong, you'd better be a whole lot brighter at sixty than you are at thirty. That means you've got to add a to-learn list to your to-do list and get busy crossing things off. It also means that if you haven't learned something really exciting in the last six weeks, you're already in deep weeds.

• **Don't worry. You'll get it.** We've all suffered anxiety attacks after watching a fourteen-year-old explain a software upgrade. But the truth is that you'll get it. We learn in fits and starts. What seems like so much spaghetti one minute suddenly becomes perfectly discernible the next. What we need is the key insight that carries us from confusion to clarity. (Unfortunately, thirty seconds before the insight arrives, our stress level is in the stratosphere and we're hoping there's still an opening at McDonald's.) Just remember, 90 percent of adult learning challenges are emotional. You can get past the intellectual hurdles if you take three deep breaths, count to ten, and look at it again.

- **Go deep, and go wide.** We can't learn everything about everything, but don't err on the side of trying to learn everything about such a narrow slice of life that you become one-dimensional. A lot can be gained by exploring disciplines unrelated to ministry. At the very least, it exposes you to different schools of thought and different problem-solving approaches. Peter Drucker chooses a new topic to study every two years. Though his most notable contributions have been in the field of management, his present passion is Japanese art.

Letting the Lunatics Run the Asylum

We can rightly talk about the ministry belonging to the Lord and the people. But we are wrong if we talk about it belonging to us. It's not our church, they are not our kids, and it's not our ministry. One of my mantras, borrowed from Bear Valley Baptist Church, is the following:

- You (the adults in the church) don't need permission to do ministry. You have been given permission from Jesus Christ.
- I, and any other Christian for that matter, have the right to demand that you do something.
- I will be your biggest cheerleader, provided
    1. you don't get into doctrinal trouble (if you do, I have to get involved);
    2. you don't ask the church for any money (if you do, I have to keep track of how you spend it, which will slow you down more than sugar in your gas tank);
    3. you don't ask for any of my time (I already have a ministry; besides, if you want to start a Boy Scout troop or a soup kitchen and you ask me to show up at the organizational meeting, everyone will look to me—not you—to lead it); and
    4. you don't expect me to keep it alive (when you get tired of the soup kitchen, it is your and God's responsibility to find your replacement). I will actively recruit folks for my projects and will help you recruit people for yours, but I'm not the one to find the leader for your project. That person needs internal motivation. If they lack it, the first time something goes south, he or she will try to throw it back in my lap.

Mail

Today's mail doesn't contain anything urgent—urgent stuff comes via the fax, phone, beeper, or Internet—so delay handling it until a low point in the day. Then be prepared to take action, or today's mail will become tomorrow's pile. Open mail over the recycle bin, and make short work of it.

Better yet, avoid getting it at all. Write to Mail Preference Service, Direct Marketing Association, P.O. Box 3861, 11 West 42nd St., New York, NY 10163-3861, and ask them to remove you from the master mailing list in the sky. Be sure to send them all the various ways you receive junk mail: Mike Woodruff, Michael Woodruff, Mike and Sheri Woodruff, Mike Woodriff, Rev. Mike Woodruff, and so on. It takes several months before you see any effect; also, while it purges you from all the lists you're currently on, it doesn't keep you off new lists. When you fill out an application for a Wally's T-Shirt World Visa Card, you can bet Wally himself will sell your name. Then you're back in the system.

Meetings

There will be about 11 million meetings in the world today (Edward E. Scannell in the foreword to *The Executive's Guide to Meetings, Conferences, and Audiovisual Presentations*). Your attendance will be required at about half of them, which means you need a few shortcuts.

• **Have a purpose.** I know this is a novel idea, but some people find it helpful to have an actual reason to meet as opposed to meeting because "it's Monday morning and we always meet on Monday morning." Step back and examine your purpose; is a meeting the best way to accomplish it? For example, meetings are good places to discuss issues but aren't very efficient ways to gather or relay information. If all you plan to do is talk, send a memo, letter, e-mail message, or fax, and save everyone some time.

• **KISS (Keep It Small, Stupid).** The larger the meeting, the more formal it will become, the more hidden agendas you'll face, the less you'll accomplish, and the more people you'll have to buy doughnuts for. Invite only people who need to be there, and give some leeway to those who want to be there and have the ability to wreak havoc if they're not invited. After people make their contributions at the meeting, let them leave.

• **Reschedule.** If the key players don't show up within ten minutes of starting time, find them or reschedule. There is no reason to discuss things you can't act upon and no reason to punish people who were on time.

• **Keep some financial perspective.** Once a year, figure out how much each minute of your meetings cost. (Start with a person's annual salary. Add about 30 percent to this number to estimate the cost of providing insurance, retirement, training, computer equipment, and so on. Then divide by two thousand, the average number of hours a person works each year. Warning: You may find that you would make more money working at McDonald's.) Churches are notorious for having four-hundred-dollar meetings to decide twenty-five-dollar matters. I've attended fund-raising meetings that took up so much time that we would have done better simply by staying at work and donating our income.

• **Distribute an agenda (see "Supplement on Agendas" on p. 57).** Preparation makes up for a lack of talent, so unless you're a lot brighter than everyone thinks, take the time to prepare and distribute an agenda. The more important the meeting, the earlier you should distribute an agenda. List the starting and ending times, meeting location, and names of everyone invited. Also whittle down the docket to a manageable number of items. Most meetings fail because they attempt to cover too much. Estimate how much time you expect to spend on each topic—this helps communicate priority—and begin with the most important topic. If participants need to do background reading, send the material with the agenda. List the issues as questions to prompt attendees' thinking. For example, don't list "photocopier" on the agenda. Instead, write,

1. Should we purchase a new photocopier?

Pros

• Current machine is recommended for three thousand copies per month, but we're making eight thousand.
• We could trade in the existing machine for a one-thousand-dollar credit.
• New machines have improved quality and capabilities.

Cons

• We would have to spend all our reserve and raise an additional seven hundred dollars.
• We'd have to delay purchasing a new computer.

Options

• We could start outsourcing large jobs to the local copy center.

Please read enclosed promotional material on two new models. Also try to think of other solutions—could we request a donation from a local business, for example?

• **Start on time.** There are lots of gimmicks for getting people to show up on time—everything from starting meetings at odd times, locking the doors once you begin, covering the most important information first, or making the last one in the room responsible for cleanup. But in the end, your reputation gets people there on time. Run no-nonsense meetings that start and end as advertised, and people will show up. Some teams form covenants asking everyone to show up on time, and post them on the wall. I've found it just as effective, and often much easier, to privately confront chronic late arrivers with a request that they try harder. Often they're not aware of just how frustrating their delayed arrival is. Another effective trick involves moving the meetings to the later person's house or office. As a last resort, you might rethink the person's position on the team. Of course, if you're going to make a big deal out of starting on time, you can't be late yourself.

• **Stop on time.** How? Schedule meetings for a room that is only available for an hour, stop discussion once people start repeating themselves, or meet standing up. People are much more likely to get to the point when they're standing up than when they're leaning back in a cushioned chair, drinking coffee, and doodling on their agendas.

• **Distribute marching orders.** Because the real test of a meeting is not discussion or planning, but results, you should never end a meeting without deciding what the next step is, who is going to take it, and when it will be accomplished. Written minutes or action plans, kept, posted, and distributed, can help. It also pays to drop short notes to people right after a meeting to say, "Just wanted to confirm that you are going to do X by 9 a.m. next Tuesday. Thanks for your help. Please see me right away if this is a problem."

Supplement on Agendas
Meeting Agenda
TO: Sheri Lynn, Karen Boyd, Ben Michaels, and Ralph Allen
FROM: Austin Conley
RE: Monthly Ministry Council Meeting
DATE: 7 p.m. to 8:30 p.m. on Thursday, June 11
LOCATION: Church library

7-7:10 Devotion by Ben
7:10-7:20 Youth pastor's update
7:20-7:40 Budget review. We're currently $2,250 in the red due to van and copier repair. Please review enclosed budget, and be prepared to discuss options.
    a. Fund-raiser—what, when, and who?
    b. Cancel rafting trip?
    c. Other
7:40-8 Intern selection update
    a. Be prepared to offer suggestions for application questions.
    b. We need to finalize salary package (tentative draft enclosed).
    c. We need to finalize job description (tentative description enclosed).

8-8:15 Photocopier—our present copier is rated for 8,000 copies per month, and we're making more than 12,500.

 a. Do we upgrade? See enclosed material for prices, options, service contracts, etc.

 b. Do we set limits for other church departments' use of our copier?

 c. Other

8:15-8:30 Miscellany

 a. Approve youth pastor's vacation schedule.

 b. Concert update

 c. Items to discuss at next meeting

Notes: Ralph, it's your turn to bring snacks.

I've scheduled a brainstorming meeting for June 20 at my house. We'll discuss ways to start our junior high program. Please block out between 7 p.m. and 9 p.m.

Mentors

A college commencement speaker once asked his graduates, "Are you smarter today than you were four years ago?" In one voice they replied "yes." Then he asked, "Will you know more twenty years from now than you do today?" Again from across the sea of black caps and gowns came one word: "yes." "Good," he said, "then go home tonight, and ask your parents for advice. They've got twenty years on all of you." You get my point. There are no smart pills to help us make wise decisions—only the Holy Spirit, experience, and friends. So after you've prayed for God's guidance, jot down the names of ten men and women whose wisdom and life skills you value. Then start inviting each of them for a cup of coffee, and see where things head. Not everyone makes a good mentor, but you need one and God has someone out there for you to learn from.

Ministries

Almost all of us are better at starting things than we are at ending them, so we wind up with all manner of programs that ceased being effective shortly after the Civil War. Now, how do we end them?

Years ago Robert Townsend suggested that every company hire a vice president in charge of killing things—an executive to wander around asking people what they're doing and why. Give a bad answer or describe a program that was good instead of great, and the project would be snuffed on the spot.

Since you probably can't get funding for such a staff person—those vice presidents have big benefits packages—you'll have to play the part yourself.

• Write down three programs—not people—that should be eliminated. Then set out to find a graceful way to end them. Some people throw a party to celebrate the good that came from a program before they end it.

• Teach the difference between basic ministries and target ministries. The former—youth ministry, small groups, nursery—are organic to the life of the church. Without them things go south. The latter come and go. God may inspire someone to start a Boy Scout troop, counsel pregnant teens, or staff a soup kitchen. If that person leaves, it's God's responsibility—not yours—to find a replacement. You don't want a bevy of target ministries staffed by halfhearted people who are only serving because you begged them to.

• Better yet, don't start programs, start pilots. You may think your idea is great, but if it doesn't take, you'll be looking for a graceful exit. On one occasion, I mobilized a lot of people and money for a seeker service on a local college campus. The service bombed. Thankfully a church leader had convinced me to call it a pilot program. We declared our test a success and the program a failure and shut it down—and we actually looked like we knew what we were doing.

Mobilizing Volunteers

Your job description—not the forty-eight-page description written by the senior pastor, but the real one found in the Bible—is only seven words long: "Prepare God's people for works of service."

That's it. The sum total. No van repair, pulpit supply, or kitchen cleanup. The Apostle Paul got right to the point. Work yourself out of a job. Recruit and train other people to do youth ministry. Set in motion something that doesn't rely on you to keep it running. In short, mobilize volunteers.

Of course that's seldom done.

But the hang-ups are not what you might guess. It has nothing to do with a lack of talent in the labor pool. In fact, to suggest that we fail because there are no dedicated, energetic, and talented laypeople around to help is to miss the point by way more than a mile. Your church is full of them. Without even knowing where you serve, I can promise you have an abundance of exciting, bright, capable, creative, and responsible people. Just look at the kind of passion and zeal they bring to their hobbies. The problem with volunteers is not the volunteers; it's the paid staff.

For years churches have complained that not enough people do the work. And for years the best and brightest people have left the church to serve in parachurch groups. Why? All the reasons point back to us.

We have to kick out the sides and stop thinking small. While hitting up the local Rotary Club for money for a drop-in shelter, I had a thirty-minute chat with the regional governor for Rotary International (the grand pooh-bah himself). This very talented man was spending an entire year traveling from one Rotary meeting to the next. And—get this—he was doing it all for free. He was donating his money and time to advance the cause of the Rotary Club.

Have you ever considered asking an established professional to spend one year of his or her life volunteering to help you? Someone did, and because he was asked—and because he considered the work worthy of his time—he said yes.

We think too small and define our work too narrowly to mobilize volunteers the way we should. Parachurch groups often attract the best and brightest because they call people to change the world. Chuck Colson, CEO of Prison Fellowship, says they have no lack of volunteers and they "think the key is to make certain [volunteers] are challenged. They get out of the narrow confines of some churches, where they've done all the volunteer tasks and still feel unfulfilled. They go to the hospitals, nursing homes, prisons, and skid row and rediscover the gospel they've been taught for so many years. They see it working in the lives of people in totally different cultures—that's spiritually explosive."

The grander the challenge—assuming you have the leadership savvy to pull it off—the easier it is to get people excited about helping out.

Musicians

If the church staff were the NBA, then the worship leader would be Dennis Rodman. An audacious statement? Maybe. But true. And it's not hair or tattoos that make them alike, although a few guitar leaders might actually give Mr. "Bad as I Want to Be" a run for the rainbow. The similarities revolve around talent. Quirky talent. Unique, attention-stealing, moody talent that is absolutely necessary to "win" but almost impossible to coach.

Managing musicians can be one of the more sizable challenges of your career. And because worship is such a critical piece of today's youth culture, the worship leader is one of the very first people to join a ministry team. That means you face a steep hill without a lot of time to build leadership momentum.

• **No two are alike.** Now before I am accused of being just the kind of left-brained, tone-deaf management geek musical types detest, let me say that not all musicians are difficult to work with. Some are the most wonderful, talented, and humble people you could ever hope to be around. They will affirm and support your leadership, deflect attention away from themselves and toward the Lord, and generate dynamic spiritual moments for those who choose to enter into worship with them. If you are fortunate enough to have such people on your staff, immediately put down this book and take them out to lunch. Shower them with thanks. Offer them your parking space, your firstborn, and half your salary. Also be sure to mention that you'd like them to commit to working with you for, oh, another thirty years.

But don't count on finding many people like that out there. The very fact that you're looking for a worship *leader* means you want someone with strong convictions, good people skills, and well-developed ideas. These people usually take charge better than they take orders. If you like to give orders, then they will not like you. One of the first things we must do is accept that what will have to change is our expectations, not their personalities. Then we're in a better position to understand, appreciate, and coach musicians.

• **Understand the Samson syndrome.** A friend of mine recently reread the story of Samson and decided that Israel's Arnold Schwarzenegger got a bad rap. Born with the strength of ten men, young Samson was always the fastest, strongest, and best at any activity requiring physical prowess. "If I was that much better than everyone else," my friend suggested, "I'd have been such a pompous, conceited jerk that I'd have made Samson look like a Boy Scout."

My feeling is that musicians—especially those who are both young and talented—face the same set of humility hurdles that Samson did. They are gifted in an area that moves people, and the church capitalizes on that. We put them in front of their peers and ask them to lead people into the presence of God Almighty. Tens, hundreds, and sometimes thousands of people respond to their direction. If you haven't been there

Myourself, you may not understand the rush such power provides.

That's why one of our jobs is to help musicians stay grounded. On more than a few occasions, I have taken musicians aside and expressed my concern for their souls. I've told them they're so good musically and so appreciated by so many people that they are almost guaranteed to take their eyes off Christ and to get warped views of themselves. No one likes to be corrected, but every musician I have spoken with expressed thanks. I think they're more aware of the dangers than I am.

- **Focus on the purpose.** One way to keep everyone grounded is to be clear about the purpose of music. If it's all about setting the right mood or drawing a big crowd, then you are talking about music, not worship. The challenges you face revolve solely around finding someone who likes your style of music, who you can get along with, and who has enough talent to advance your agenda. But if the goal is worship—and most of the time it had better be—then you are after someone who can help your group learn how to corporately enter into the presence of the Creator. This requires an additional set of requirements. You still need someone who likes your group's style of music and who has musical talent, but you also need someone with a worshipper's heart. He or she must be playing for an audience of One. This is a find.

- **Share your heart.** Effective worship leaders are sensitive people, and that means they will be tuned into your emotional and spiritual state more than many others around you. It also means they'll be some of the first to see through any fronts you put on. Don't expect them to be excited about working with you if you're not growing closer to Christ yourself. And don't expect them to stay around very long if you're not helping to shepherd their souls.

- **Work the logistics.** Time is a problem for volunteer worship leaders. They need to practice on their own, and they need to practice with others in the group. This type of heavy commitment often precludes small-group study time, which can be OK if the practice sessions are not just about music. The sessions should truly revolve around Christ, and someone should disciple the group.

- **Admenistrayshun.** No, that is not a typo. I butchered the word "administration" to make a point. Most musicians don't know how to spell it. The creative, emotional energy that makes them so valuable with guitars seems to subvert any chance that they are wired with much organizational savvy. Some are! (Hey, you may have it much better than you know.) But many are not, and that means they may need help.

Some groups appoint a worship leader and a worship administrator. The latter helps the former pull together details like actually having the right overheads for the songs they will sing. Other churches spend more time developing a master calendar that spells out many of the details way in advance. Still others just make certain to

hold a premeeting huddle to talk through the program a few days before the large group meeting or Sunday morning service.

• **Deal with succession.** After three years of providing unmatched worship leadership, Chuck Clarke did something only a few college students ever manage: He graduated. Once we were over the surprise, we realized we were in deep weeds. And in fact, the next six to nine months were awful. Chuck had not done a great job replacing himself, and I hadn't really bothered to make sure he did. But that mistake only happened once. After that, we started aggressively recruiting freshman so we would always have leaders. We even began offering group guitar lessons and, in some cases, helped promising people buy additional equipment. You must make certain that you develop worship leaders.

• **Keep it fresh.** If your musicians are locked into the same old songs, send them to other churches or youth groups to learn new ones. Today's musical trends are as dynamic as tastes are eclectic, and you simply must rotate in new songs.

• **Keep it legal.** If the FBI ever decides to prosecute churches for copyright violations, they'll have to build a penitentiary at least as large as California to hold all the youth ministers. It should not be that way. Make certain you're in compliance with federal laws governing music.

Networking

Once every twelve to eighteen months, I learn something that changes my life. Most of the time, it's something others learned in fifth grade, which leads me to suspect that I spent too much time at recess. But since most youth pastors majored in recess, you probably don't know this stuff either.

Recently I've learned the power of networking. Simply stated, it's not *what* you know, it's *who* you know. For much of my life, I worked very hard. Now I talk on the phone and get more done. It's not a bad life, and I think everyone wins.

Example 1: A college student I know broke into a vacant university building on a dare. To his surprise—though to no one else's—he managed to set off a silent alarm. When the police showed up, he hid in a closet. When the police dogs showed up, he got caught. Because the building was a historical site, he was going to get clobbered with a felony. His parents hired attorneys. When he came to see me, I picked up the phone and called a law enforcement official, a friend, and said, "I know this kid. He's an idiot, but he's not a felon." My friend said, "OK. If he'll do X, Y, and Z, we'll work to keep this off his record." It was over in forty-eight hours.

Example 2: I spent a month begging Coca-Cola to send a speaker to our college ministry conference. (I wanted to know how they track trends among youth and what they thought the next generation would be like.) After all my efforts failed, I ran into a friend who said, "I know the West Coast regional sales director for Coke. Let me see what he can do." Four phone calls later, I was taking a bath in Sprite.

Example 3: When trying to arrange a meeting between Amy Grant and a friend fighting cancer, my assistant called a dozen people, sent lots of faxes, and dashed off enough e-mail messages to shut down AOL—all in a full-scale effort to break through the palace guards and get noticed. Suddenly I remembered that I knew a guy who knew a guy who knew Amy. Two phone calls later, the backstage passes arrived.

Harvey Mackay, a management speaker whose first book, *Swim With the Sharks,* was a huge bestseller, also wrote "Dig Your Well Before You Are Thirsty," which is about networking. In it, he suggests that the entire world is informally linked by, at most, six degrees of separation. (You know someone who knows someone who knows someone who knows someone who knows someone who can get you in touch with who you need to talk to.) Mackay also suggests that the people who have won the game of life are those who have the biggest Rolodexes. (Not too surprisingly, Mackay's is the size of Rhode Island, and he claims to be able to reach anyone in the world in just three calls.)

Mackay dedicates at least one hour a day and four hours on Sundays to networking. For no reason other than staying in touch, he calls friends and acquaintances to catch up. He learns as much as he can about them and serves them as often as he can so that when he needs a favor, he can call in the chips.

You already have a network. It consists of your family, friends, classmates, and neighbors. The goal is to be a bit more intentional in who you know and in how you interact so you can contact these people for help later on.

- **Start your list.** Every night before going to bed, Bill Clinton writes down the name of every new person he met that day as well as a few things about that person. He adds those cards to his database so he can stay in touch as needed. Rolodexes are made for this, though contact software is even better.

- **Study your list.** Are you impressed? Do you have the people on the list that you need to? Are there doctors and attorneys? teachers and school administrators? coaches? police officers? Work to expand your network. Volunteer for community boards. Make friends outside of your usual circles. Work to develop a cross section of people who you will be able to leverage to serve others.

- **Stay in touch.** Program your software to remind you to call people once every quarter (or month, year, etc.). When you run across an article that reminds you of someone, send him or her a copy. When you travel to a friend's hometown, bring back a copy of the hometown newspaper. Invite to dinner a couple of different people who don't know each other just to have a lively conversation. Send cards just to say hello.

- **Serve.** Many people use their network to get ahead; however, if you approach this opportunity with a one-sided mind-set, it will not take you far. If you hope others will one day be able to help you, then you need to help them.

- **Know what to know.** After you commit to building up your Rolodex, determine just what it is you want to know about people. Since this is your database, I'll let you decide. But a handful of fairly standard entries include: name, spouse's name, kids' names and ages, occupation, address, phone, e-mail, birthday, last time you spoke, interests and hobbies, hometown, college(s), and affiliations.

No

Learn to say this word—and often, especially to yourself. If you find that you're not saying it often enough to other people, try these tricks:

- Don't say "yes," say, "Let me think about it."
- Ask, "May I have your permission to say 'no'? I am simply running too thin right now."
- Hand them the phone and say, "You call my family and tell them I'm signing up for something else. I don't have the guts."

The Non-Negotiables for Administrative Assistants

- **They love Christ.** Your assistants do not have to be members of your church—in fact, there are advantages if they're not—but they do need to love Christ. How else can they be part of your ministry team?

- **They love kids.** Ditto point one. These people set the tone of the office. Next to piping organ music into the area, the most effective way to keep kids away is to hire an assistant who can't stand anyone younger than age twenty-five.

- **They are low-maintenance.** People with significant personal needs have a place in the church, but not on your ministry team. After all, hospitals don't hire sick people, they admit them.

- **They can keep secrets.** Within weeks, your assistants will have enough dirt on enough people to do serious damage to your work. My staff teams, including assistants, have all drafted covenants that, among other things, include a commitment to confidentiality.

- **They are loyal.** You need someone in your corner. That might mean speaking up on your behalf or defending the youth program in general. It certainly means coming directly to you—and not to anyone else—if you've done something wrong or if they have complaints.

- **They can be fired.** Don't hire the board chairman's son, the choir director's mother, or anyone else you can't dismiss without starting a civil war. And think long and hard before hiring your spouse. He or she may be the best one for the job, but it will be harder than ever to have a life outside of work.

- **They are competent where it counts.** Do you want a warm, friendly voice and surrogate counselor or a bookkeeper to make sense out of red ink and carwash money? Many churches want both without realizing that most accountants are a bit shy on warmth and charm. Identify your most critical needs, and hire accordingly.

- **They are above reproach.** Familiarity breeds contempt, but just as often it breeds opportunity. This is why many bosses run off with their secretaries—pastors included. Be wise and cautious. Give your spouse veto power over who you hire, though don't advertise this or you'll get yourself sideways with the EEOC. Also don't hire anyone you're attracted to or who you think is immature enough to have a crush on you.

Nonprofit

Without intending to embarrass anyone, I would like to set the record straight. In the eyes of the state, being a nonprofit institution does not mean you may not make a profit on an event such as a ski weekend or mission trip. It does not imply that you should lose money on fund-raisers or keep a zero balance in your checking account. It doesn't prohibit you from selling T-shirts for more than they cost you to make or buy, nor does it threaten you with jail time if you have more money at the end of the year than you had at the beginning. Being nonprofit means that

• no investors are making money from your work—you don't sell shares in your youth group as Microsoft does on the NASDAQ—and

• you're subject to certain restrictions on what types of salaries can be paid (trust me, you're well below the danger level).

I'm convinced that many people who thrive in ministry could make boatloads of money in business. However, an equal number would be bankrupt by noon. The love of money is the root of all sorts of evil. Having a positive cash flow for your ministry is not.

Performance Reviews

Do you know what I think about you? What I really, deep down in my heart, think about the job you're doing?

Of course not. I haven't told you. And until I do, all you can do is guess.

Now for the important question: Does your staff know what you think about them? their performance? their strengths and weaknesses? how you think they could improve?

Not unless you've told them. And chances are you haven't. Most managers—and this means you if a paid or volunteer staff reports to you—spend more time sharpening mechanical pencils than they do giving feedback. It's not that they fail to evaluate; it's that they fail to communicate what they're thinking. They stop short of sharing their insights in a way that could help their staff grow in effectiveness. It's a crime.

Most of us in ministry are not wired to give performance reviews. We are "nice" people in a "nice" line of work. Telling people they're not doing a nice job is…well, it's not nice. But people unable or unwilling to do their jobs must be confronted. That is *your* job. And the more quickly you deal with problem situations, the better off everyone is.

• **The team member is better off** because he or she receives the coaching deserved. People who work for what you pay them or volunteer their time for free are there because they want to do a good job. They deserve all the help you can offer them. (Coaches get people to do things they've never wanted to do in order to become who they've always wanted to be.)

• **You are better off** because your stress level drops two hundred points. Few things sap us of energy more quickly than unresolved conflict.

• **Your other staff members are better off** because they see that what they do matters. By confronting those who do little or nothing, you validate the efforts of those who do contribute.

• **The church is better off** because the job gets done and team morale is higher. Additionally, the church is spared the nightmares that can occur when unresolved conflict erupts.

Also remember that feedback is the breakfast of champions. As a leader, it's your job to coach your team. Performance reviews don't have to be ugly. Think of it this way: In tennis and golf, we call performance reviews "lessons," and people pay a lot of money to take them. Youth ministry may not be a sporting event, but you are a "pro" and it is your job to help those around you become as good, if not better, than you are. Next to hiring the right people, conducting effective performance reviews is your most important managerial task. Here are the basics:

• **As a team leader, you need to start by winning the right to be heard.** Though you can pull rank, you'll be far more effective if you start by convincing your staff that you are committed to their success more than to your own. Listen to their ideas, and praise them in front of their peers. Frequently refer to their successes in your messages, and you'll validate their ministry to every listener.

• **Work to create a culture in which performance reviews are natural.** This means not only welcoming criticism of your own performance, but also telling potential team members that they'll be periodically reviewed.

• **Tailor reviews to fit your staff.** New staff members need more feedback than those who have been with you longer, but every member of your team deserves three types of input.

1. Spontaneous—Sooner is almost always better than later. When you see people doing something well, let them know. When you see them doing something wrong, tell them then. Don't wait unless you have to.

2. Monthly—You should meet individually with each team member at least once a month to hear how they're doing. This keeps your people focused on high-priority tasks and allows you to stay current with their progress.

3. Annually—Once a year, summarize each staff member's contributions. The goal is to help staff wrap up the year and get ready for the future. If you bring up new information at this point, then you've failed earlier.

Planning Retreats

Periodically the leadership of every group needs to step back and think, to strategize and assess, to pray and plan. That is what retreats are for.

Take out whatever scraps of paper you use for a calendar, and mark out two solid days for a planning retreat. You and the youth group brain trust will set aside forty-eight hours to schedule trouble for the entire year.

• **Where?** It doesn't really matter. I've attended planning retreats in ski lodges, hotel rooms, church basements, summer homes, and so on. You'll need room to sit, access to food, the nonnegotiable creature comforts such as water and bathrooms, and the ability to hide from church members and avoid all phone calls. Church members' summer homes are ideal; they're free and far enough away that you can avoid bumping into someone you know.

• **When?** Last month would have been ideal, but we'll settle for any time you can get the right people away for at least two days and one night. I actually prefer three days and two nights, but given your schedule, we'll achieve peace on earth first. Spring is a good time to plan for the following year, because school is winding down and you have plenty of lead time before the fall schedule kicks in.

• **Who?** You and your team. Spouses are great. Kids—the ones you work with and the ones with your last name—aren't.

• **What are the guidelines?** As a consultant, I've developed a list of "rules" that I impose on the groups I'm working with. You're free to borrow any of the following or to make up your own.

Keep in mind the one-hundred-mile rule. No one can leave the meeting or even take a phone call for anything they wouldn't drive one hundred miles to deal with.

The goal is consensus. It's impossible to get everyone to agree on everything, but everyone must be willing and able to offer his or her complete support—with vigor—once the meeting ends. (If they can't, we're not finished.)

Silence equals consent. People must speak their minds. If someone disagrees with the direction the group is going, they must say so.

Seek first to understand, then to be understood. Enough said.

The overall ministry's needs must be the focus. Members of the leadership team may have their own areas of expertise—worship, Sunday school, ministry at a certain high school—but expect them to think more like members of a senior management team, not like department heads.

Attack problems, not people. Conflict is inevitable and should be embraced, but it must be dealt with in a timely and mature manner.

• **Plan the retreat.** I know that planning a planning event appears a bit anal, but you really will need a tight agenda to maximize the time. You'll want to publish a

"...and this one is for chaperoning the Lock-In of '93;
this one is for heroism—during the 26 hours I was
tied to a bunk at the '95 Fall retreat..."

rough draft of the agenda at least two weeks before the event. Here are my notes. Plagiarize at will.

Wednesday

3 p.m.—Catch the ferry to Orcas Island. (Note: When you copy someone else's paper, you need to change a few details so it's not too obvious what you're doing. You don't have to go to Orcas Island.)

5 p.m.—Arrive at the cabin and get settled.

6 p.m.—Eat dinner.

7 p.m.—Begin group introductions. Everyone must interview one member of the team, learn something new about that person, and share it with the group.

8 p.m.—Discuss change. Brainstorm the following questions:

- *What five biggest changes have we experienced in the past three years?*
- *What five areas do we expect to change most in the next five years?*
- *What five areas do we expect will never change?*

9 p.m.—Play cards or a board game.

Thursday

7 a.m.—Eat breakfast and have a devotion. (Note: Rotate the food prep, cleanup, and devotions.)

8 a.m.—Begin with prayer.

8:20 a.m.—To team build, take a quick, self-scoring personality test and let everyone guess everyone else's score.

10 a.m.—Take a break.

10:30 a.m.—Two-plus-one: Everyone shares two affirmations and one challenge for each person in the group. They do so in front of the group, and the person receiving the feedback listens until everyone has responded.

12 p.m.—Break for lunch.

1:30 p.m.—Assess. Focus on the standard four questions of all organizational assessments:

- *What are we doing well?*
- *What are we doing but doing poorly?*
- *What are we not doing that we should be?*
- *What could blow us out of the water if we don't address it?*

3:30 p.m.—Break until dinner. Have a group activity such as wally-ball.

5:30 p.m.—Eat dinner. During dinner take some time for each group member to share his or her greatest success story. I suggest this because organizations—and especially the type A personalities who run them—often don't celebrate their successes. It's great for the whole group to remember and be encouraged by what God has done through each person.

6:30 p.m.—Begin strategic planning and strategic intent. Strategic planning, by definition, is a statement of where you are headed based on where you have been. Look at the past three years for any trends—are you getting bigger or smaller? gaining volunteers or losing them? gaining church members or losing them? Much of the information you gather can and should be plotted on a graph. Strategic intent, on the flip side, is a statement of where you want to go. It ignores the past and simply looks to the future with questions such as

- *If we knew we couldn't fail, what would we be attempting to do for God?*
- *What do we believe God wants done within our sphere of influence?*
- *What would we like the group to look like in three years?*

9 p.m.—Play games.

Friday

7 a.m.—Eat breakfast and have a devotion.

8 a.m.—Draft a team covenant. A covenant is a collection of guidelines very similar to the off-site ground rules, but they carry forward after the retreat ends. The covenant, which you will only be able to start, is designed to uncover people's unwritten expectations about how they deal with one another.

10 a.m.—Have a break.

10:30 a.m.—Establish key measurement areas (KMAs). Organizations often find it helpful to establish and track five to ten KMAs. Your list might include the obvious, such as attendance, decisions for Christ, and money in the bank, but be sure it includes other mission-critical variables such as a number of adult volunteers.

12 p.m.—Eat lunch.

1:30 p.m.—Plan the year. Buy a huge wall calendar or hand out 8 1/2x11-inch calendars to everyone; then mark up the entire year. Be sure someone has a calendar that captures all of last year's events. This, along with your strategic intent, is your starting point.

3 p.m.—Develop a communication plan. Before you head home, consider how you will share the information you've talked about. Some of the team-building exercises may have led to confidential information. Many of the vision items may be best kept as leadership "secrets" for now. The decisions are up to you, but you probably need to spend some time discussing who is going to say what and when.

4 p.m.—Head home. (Hurry, the 5 p.m. ferry won't wait.)

If you're half as bright as you claim—and therefore three times as smart as your senior pastor believes you to be—you'll know that this is an aggressive agenda. I offer it only as a start. The key is to get away, meet with one another and God, and plan the year.

Planning Your Schedule

Given twenty ticks of the clock to get something done, the best use of the first five is to plan the next fifteen. Planning time saves time. I've found that a fourfold attack works best:

• Two hours every December, while everyone else is mulling over his or her resolutions, sit down with your old calendar and transfer any reoccurring events into your new date book. Our lives are far more cyclical than we think, and last year's schedule is an invaluable tool for planning the upcoming year.

• Keep a tickler file for each month of the year. I file staff agendas, budgets, critiques of reoccurring events, and other assorted memos in these folders. Thirty minutes each month, delve into the file. By leafing through your notes from last June, you'll be better able to plan for this June.

• One hour each week, sit down and plan the week. I now use an electronic calendar, so much of what I used to do—transferring upcoming events from my monthly calendar to my daily calendar, for example—is now done for me. But I still review my appointments and action items as well as glance at my goals. It helps me to jump-start on Monday morning.

• Twenty minutes every day, plan for the following day. Planning used to be the first thing on my docket each morning, but now every afternoon before I leave for home, I plan for the next day. Then I leave the office feeling as if I'm not completely insane. It also ensures that I can jump right into my most important tasks first thing in the morning, without wasting my best time of the day on planning what I should be doing.

Post-Wedding Counseling

I started requiring a post-wedding checkup for couples once I realized how little they learned in premarital counseling. Requiring a follow-up session, which typically occurs a couple of months after the wedding, as part of their premarital counseling erases any embarrassment that might be attached to it.

Pre-Engagement Counseling

I started offering pre-engagement classes in addition to typical premarital counseling once I realized how hard it was to talk anyone with a ring on his or her finger out of a bad match. This was also prompted by learning—to my horror—that some couples were getting engaged earlier than they'd planned just so they could take the premarital classes when they were offered.

Premarital Counseling

There is a lot of great premarital counseling material for you to plagiarize. I offer only two pieces of additional advice.

• **Draft a premarital-purity covenant.** During your first meeting with the future bride and groom, ask them to draft an agreement they will sign and then hand back to you. It will list what they will and will not do sexually between now and the wedding. This not only sets limits, but also provides an easy way to hold them accountable to righteous standards. (I occasionally return the covenant after their wedding rehearsal and suggest that they rip it up and burn the pieces.)

• **Have the sex talk.** It's easy to assume that everybody—including the kids in your junior high group—is having sex more often than the elders in your church, but by God's grace at least a few aren't. Those who do save themselves for marriage deserve the best start we can give them. Thus, the talk. During the last session of premarital counseling, I sit down with the groom and my wife sits down with the bride for a frank, no-questions-barred session. I almost stopped offering these talks because of the awkward moments leading up to them—I'd rather speak to five hundred kids about sex than to one—but the truth is that they don't know the truth. And who else can they ask?

Priorities

Gordon MacDonald *(Ordering Your Private World)* wrote about the "Essential, the Necessary and the Urgent." Charles Hummel discussed the same things in his best-selling pamphlet, "The Tyranny of the Urgent." Steven Covey *(The Seven Habits of Highly Effective People)* preaches about living in Quadrant Two. All three men make the same critical point: The most important things in life are seldom the most urgent. In fact, unimportant but deadline-driven tasks often squeeze out the things that are truly important but not urgent. Effective people know this and fight this tendency like a wild hyena. Focus your time and attention on what matters, not on what's screaming the loudest.

Pushing Paper

It's just before five when you push open your office door and scan your desk, shelves, and floor for a place to set a box of fliers. Since the organizational fairy hasn't yet arrived, there isn't a free square inch in sight. You're still rehearsing your options when the phone rings, so you balance the fliers on top of the volleyball nets and answer the phone. It's the church treasurer demanding a financial report. Of course, since the report fairy also didn't show, that isn't finished either. "I've got to get those numbers from you by 5 p.m., or you won't be reimbursed until I get back from vacation. Do you have my fax number?" You've taken it down every month for two years but have a better chance of nailing Jell-O to a tree than finding it, so you say "no" and start rifling through three desk drawers looking for scrap paper. Finally you give up, and write the number on your hand. That done, you pick up a stack of mail from your chair—the secretary couldn't find anywhere else to set it—and plop down. You've got to find the numbers for the report, but you glance through the mail first. Three pieces look important, so you wedge the rest into a small, overflowing wastebasket and look for a spot to set the good stuff. You don't dare throw it on top of one of the existing stacks—you might not find it for years—so you clear a space by combining two of the smaller piles. While you work to make sure the new pile won't topple over—stacks over four feet tall do require a good base—you realize that all of these piles are made up of "important" papers. In fact, everything on your desk is there because at one time or another, you thought it was important. You're feeling pretty low when you realize you've unearthed a few of the receipts you need for the financial report, so you turn and bolt for the fax machine. It's only 5:11. If you hurry—and fabricate the numbers you don't have—you just might make it. Unfortunately, on the way out the door, your shoe hooks the volleyball net and you pull the box of fliers all over the floor.

I could go on, but I'll spare us all the pain. Suffice it to say that you got this job because of your good looks, not your administrative savvy. And besides, it's not your fault: You were promised a paperless office! In its place you find a tornado of notes, spreadsheets, and mail.

What to do? Start by accepting the ugly but undeniable facts:

• **Managing information is critical to our effectiveness.** It helps us get things done and avoid having the energy sucked out of us by all the clutter, confusion, and visual noise our random-filing-and-piling systems create.

• **Despite technological advances, paper still has a place.** Technology has changed our world, but fax machines, photocopiers, and laser printers are spitting out more paper every hour.

• **Some people manage the paper flow quite well, which means it can be done.** The goal is not a meticulous office with color-coded files neatly stacked on a clean desk. The goal is a work space that helps you do the best job in the least amount of time.

It all comes down to understanding that paper clutter means postponed decisions and paper management is decision-making. Here are my suggestions:

• **Stop it before it arrives.** Cancel subscriptions to magazines you don't read, have junk mail thrown out before it reaches your desk, and ask to be removed from routing slips you don't profit from. (Also see "Mail" on p. 55.) Be brutal. Then do your part to cut down the flow of paper traffic. Whenever possible, go electronic. When you have to write, keep it short and make it a big deal to send a copy to anyone. It takes less time and no file cabinets to talk rather than write, so talk when you can. The only items you want to consistently cut down a tree for are those that will keep you out of court—legal documents, the flow of large sums of money, and performance appraisals, for example.

• **Make decisions.** The goal is to touch a piece of paper only once; though that's unrealistic for many of us, we should never pick up a piece of paper and set it back down in the same spot, which is what most people spend thirty minutes a day doing. Don't pick up a piece of paper until you're ready to act on it. When you're ready to act, you have several options.

Sort—We all need one "sort" pile—an in-basket, a tray, or even a corner of your desk. Papers land here when they enter your office or when you don't know what to do with them. The one rule is that they can't stay. Everyone needs a permanent resting place, and this pile isn't that. In fact, you're not allowed more than one sort pile, and no piece of paper can park there overnight.

Recycle—When in doubt, throw it out. Keep a large recycle bin by your desk, and feed it more often than you feed yourself.

Refer—If the letter you're reading would interest Billy Bob, then write his name on it and send it his way. Do not set it down on your desk again.

Record—Most of what we have on little sheets of paper would be of more value recorded in our calendars, so make sure you have enough room in whatever system you use to write both your appointments and your action list. After you have transferred the relevant information, deep-six the paper.

Act—Better yet, don't record it anywhere. Just do it. When First United Church writes to ask if their youth group can sleep at your church on their way to Mexico, either pick up the phone and give them an answer or write your reply right on their letter and send it back. Don't waste your time writing them a separate letter; that could take a while, so you may put it off.

File—At the risk of sounding like a social zero, I will go on record as saying you should spend some serious time with your filing system. If, as I suspect, we're not just spiritual developers but also information brokers, then we need to be able to access information. We need a streamlined, functional system.

If this all sounds like a grand strategy, but you don't know where to get started, let me suggest two options.

• **Option 1:** Block off four hours on Friday afternoon, move a trash bin into the hallway outside your office, and have at it. The rules are simple: You can't put a piece of paper down in the same spot again, and your options are limited to recycling, referring, recording, acting, or filing. Get rid of it all. Discover office furniture you didn't know you had. Throw away eight-track tapes and pasta from those 1970s BBQs. You might even find an intern under all the rubble.

• **Option 2:** Hire someone to do it for you. Jeffery Mayer, who wrote *If You Don't Have Time to Do It Right, When Will You Have Time to Do It Again?* will gladly clean your desk. He charges just over one thousand dollars, and it takes him less than four hours. (Nice work if you can get it.)

Quitting Time

A few years ago Fortune magazine listed job-related time away from home as the number one source of executive guilt in this country. I suspect that a survey of youth pastors would produce similar findings. In fact, I suspect it would be worse. Why?

Because nothing in our world encourages us to stop working. In fact, because we don't have a standard quitting time and because evenings are part of the package, youth pastors often work until one of two things happen.

1. Their health fails.

2. Their spouses complain.

Since most of us have more energy than wisdom, our health will survive longer than our marriages.

Please realize this trap for what it is. Your job will never be finished. There will always be more you could do, more students you could call, more books you could read. And you'll get plenty of strokes for doing so. The church loves workaholic staff members; they're a great bargain. But if you don't schedule time with your family, you force your spouse to nag.

At the beginning of every month, sit down and schedule special times with your family. Write them in ink, and try to make at least some more exciting than "spend time with family." Let's face it: If we were as creative with our families as we are paid to be with our youth groups, we'd win national awards from Focus on the Family and would work a lot harder to protect those times.

Quitting: Two Views

• **Don't.** Youth ministry is littered with people who bail out as soon as a bit of water comes over the bow. Sure, parents can be unreasonable. Sure, senior pastors can be jerks. Sure, the hours are long and the pay is low. But you knew that before you took the job. (At least you should have.) Most youth ministers leave their ministries way too quickly and way too often. Which means we don't stay in one spot long enough to know what works and what doesn't. The ability to build a team, develop volunteers, track kids, and make a long-term impact takes time. So plan to stay, and don't ever leave until you feel God's release—better yet, until you feel his subtle push. And whatever you do, don't leave this job thinking that the next one will be better. Changing this church for the next one means trading problems that you know about for problems that you don't know about. And besides, wherever you end up, *you'll* still be there, which guarantees that most of the same problems will be there, too.

• **Do.** When God says you've finished, it's time to leave. Don't keep the job until something better comes along. Ministry is about a calling, not a paycheck. Furthermore, don't shop your contract like a free agent hoping for a better offer. If you are underpaid, then ask for a raise. If bad blood exists between you and some parents, deal with it. Neither are reasons to leave. The resignation question is fundamentally answered by listening to God. When God says, "It's time to go," then it's time to go. (Also see "Resigning," p. 86.)

Raises

Let me start by making three unpopular statements:

1. If money is important to you, then you took a wrong turn back in college. The ministry is for those people ready to make sacrificial commitments for eternal causes. You ought to be paid less than you could earn doing other things because then you'll be certain you serve because of a call and not a paycheck.

2. Everybody I know thinks he or she "needs" more money. Few people think they're paid what they're worth. Yet salaries are a relative thing. Everyone reading this is paid more than most citizens outside the West even dream of. But everyone knows someone else who makes more. The inequity makes us all cry foul.

3. If you receive a raise, you'll take a bigger bite out of the church's cash flow. And since that money is in your pocket, it will not be available for other uses—missions, for example. Therefore, it's important that you are not overpaid.

Now having said that—and alienating most youth pastors and their families—I will try to redeem myself. You may very well be underpaid. In fact, this is a pretty safe assumption. Relative to who we are, what we know, how hard we work, and how important our mission is, few groups are compensated as poorly as youth pastors are. There are bound to be exceptions, and the three of you who are overpaid know who you are. Furthermore, a good number of us is paid fairly. But many of us are forced to limp by on a wage that makes owning a home a joke and driving a '74 Pinto a way of life.

In your dreams the church would offer a healthy salary, a signing bonus, a car allowance, a cell phone, conference money, and other extras too numerous to mention. In a fair world, the church would make sure your salary was competitive with teachers and other professionals, and they would even occasionally raise your salary before you think to ask. But in the fallen world in which you live, you'll probably have to be your own advocate. In that light, you need to know there are right and wrong ways to go about securing a raise.

The wrong ways include whining and threatening to quit, two short-term approaches that might work in a pinch but do not represent a long-term strategy.

The right ways take much more thought:

• **Do a good job.** Before you ask for more money, ask yourself, "Am I worth it? Am I doing a substantially better job than when my salary was set? Is the group growing? Have we met the goals we set?" Outside of a cost-of-living increase, we shouldn't expect more money just because we've put in more time.

• **Educate the church.** Everyone thinks Acts 2 is a good model for determining a salary package...for someone else to follow. But with the exception of missionaries and youth pastors, most people are paid based on their performance, not on their need. You need to decide which compensation approach you want to take. When I joined a church staff back in 1985, my salary—$16,500 per year with no benefits—was based on need. No one suggested that it was fair for a seminary graduate to make less money than an employee at McDonald's, but no one held a gun to my head either. I took the job, and my wife and I lived a simple life. As time went on, we started a family and needed a bigger place to live. My salary needs went up, and the church came through. But after about four years of this, I realized that even though our ministry was growing rapidly, the only way I was going to make any more money was to have another kid or buy a bigger house. When I found myself thinking about having another child to secure a raise, I knew it was time to switch philosophies. I went to the church leaders and suggested that, outside of the Soviet Union, everyone I knew was paid based on merit. It took about eighteen months—and the fall of the USSR—but eventually they came around.

• **Establish a bench mark.** Since few people get paid what they think they're worth, you have to let the market decide. On two occasions I felt I was significantly underpaid, so I called a dozen youth pastors with ministries similar to mine and asked what their salaries were. By filling in a grid that included salary and benefits for a dozen colleagues—men and women from around town but from a variety of denominations—I was able so show that I was clearly on the low side. This information was invaluable in negotiating a salary increase.

The Senior Pastor at home

"We're in trouble, honey.
The youth pastor wants to be paid by the hour."

81

- **See the senior pastor as your ally.** When it comes to negotiating a raise, there are a number of people you should have in your corner, but few can be more important than senior pastors. They probably have the best idea of what it's like to start out in ministry and of how hard you work. Besides, if they are against a merit increase, it probably won't happen.

I've been fortunate to work under two senior pastors who lobbied hard on my behalf. One openly suggested he would be going to bat for my increase and added that in the following year he would appreciate any help I could offer when it was his turn to ask for a raise. The other made certain the committee reviewing staff salaries was made up of local employers who had close ties to the marketplace. By "stacking" the committee with people who understood that they had to pay a competitive wage for good people, he virtually guaranteed my raise.

- **Be creative.** If the church really doesn't have the money, there may be other ways to augment your income.

Moonlighting—A church that knows you qualify for food stamps is often willing to let you make money on the side. I've taught classes at the local technical school, offered seminars, written articles, and drawn cartoons to make ends meet. I've also looked long and hard at being a chaplain in the reserves. There is a multitude of options other than flipping burgers.

Bonuses—Many companies are scaling back on salaries but offering bonuses if the company performs. Our church agreed to pay the staff a healthy bonus if certain criteria were met. If the church grew and the budget was exceeded, each staff member could receive up to two thousand extra dollars at the end of the year. The program was not without its critics, but it did work. Every year it was offered, we all received close to the full bonus.

Raise support—As the college ministry grew, it became obvious that any additional salaries we needed would have to come from outside sources. Today, of eight full-time workers on the college staff, the church pays only one. The other seven raise support in much the same way a missionary does.

Reading

You can make it to thirty on good looks and personality, but if you want to finish strong, you'll have to grow mentally. That means studying and reading. Since there is more in print than you could ever hope to peruse, I offer the following shortcuts:

- **Don't try to read it all.** Most books are not worth your time. They are poorly written and say very little. Choose niches you want to master, and be selective. Have an expert steer you to the best book on a specific topic.
- **Know your goal.** If you're lounging around with a Grisham novel, just enjoy

it. But if you're reading to expand your horizons, follow your hunches. If you're reading to complete a task, then get in and get out. Skip words, focus on summary statements, and speed read.

• **Judge a book by its cover.** And by its table of contents and index as well. You should be able to spend ten minutes with a book—skimming the introduction, reading chapter summaries, glancing to see which topics are listed the most—and know if it merits more time.

• **Form a reading group.** You're not the only one who can't keep up. Divide popular journals among a few friends so each person is responsible to brief the others on the one or two best articles. The discussion is almost always better than the articles.

Other shortcuts: Read book reviews, listen to books on tape, and schedule time to read. (It really is part of your job.)

Reading Résumés

Two months after you've advertised a position for an opening on the church staff, your desk will be buried under six feet of résumés. Some will be written in crayon (I'm not kidding), and some will be written by people who are probably institutionalized (again, I'm not kidding). The rest will fall into three categories: high potential, possible, and unqualified. Send each candidate a postcard that reads, "Thank you for sending your résumé. We'll be in touch with you as our search process continues." Then start reading.

Use the selection criteria you've developed earlier (see "Hiring" on p. 43) to sort through the stack. Some experts suggest that you read each résumé from the bottom up, since people will list their best information at the beginning. Other experts warn that lots of space devoted to education or hobbies might indicate trouble; success in the classroom doesn't guarantee success outside of it, and a long list of outside interests might indicate little time for work. Tricks aside, do understand that people will make themselves look as good as they possibly can. Learn to read between the lines.

When someone says he or she has recruited, trained, and supervised Bible study leaders, that probably means the person ran an ad seeking people interested in leading studies, five people showed up, and he or she presented a two-hour crash course using someone else's material. If a candidate has built up a team of seventy-five small groups, took them through a one-year training program, and then met with them weekly for discipleship and accountability, expect some specific numbers to show up in the résumé. Also, qualifiers such as "had exposure to," "assisted with," and "have knowledge of" basically mean they have no hands-on experience in that area.

Recruiting Volunteers

Many books have been written on this topic, and unfortunately most of them are drivel. They start with the assumption that you are asking people to do you a favor by donating their time. Yet that is clearly not the attitude of any of the world's revolutionaries, including Christ. Study their tactics, and you'll see they believed in their causes so strongly that they expected others to get involved. To be a Christian is to serve.

- **Be sure you have something for volunteers to do.** Creating hype in order to sign up a lot of people will backfire unless you're ready to plug them in.
- **Don't make general appeals.** It's better to recruit people individually or in small groups. (Oddly enough, the smaller the group, the more likely you are to find a volunteer.) Make multiple appeals to Sunday school classes rather than one big appeal to the congregation.

The Reference Check

What's been done counts a lot more than what's been said. The best indicator of what someone will do in the future is what he or she has done in the past. References help you check an applicant's past. Don't take anything for granted. If they've told you they've done something, check. And don't just consider what the reference says, but also consider who the reference is. Is this person qualified to judge? Does the applicant list his or her current supervisor? Does the applicant list people who report to him or her? Most people can find three others to speak highly of them. So who is speaking and just how high and how specific are the praises?

If the applicant lists more than three references, start with those on the bottom first since they'll probably be the most honest. Ask each reference for the names of others you could talk to, especially previous employers. And realize that people's assessment of a staff person is clarified over time, so try to locate someone for whom the candidate worked two or three situations ago. You'll get a far more honest account. If possible, meet with the references face to face, perhaps over lunch, and ask very specific questions; "Did he or she do a good job?" will not yield one-tenth the insight that "Did he or she work well with the parents of the kids in the program?" will reveal. References are not likely to volunteer unflattering information unless you ask specific questions. You shouldn't quit snooping until you know the applicant's flaws. No one's perfect except Jesus Christ.

Two warnings: In this litigious society in which many employees sue former bosses over poor recommendations, many companies will not allow their staff to give out any information on past employees beyond a verification of the applicant's position and dates of employment. This kind of stonewall should not reflect negatively on a candi-

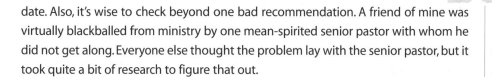

date. Also, it's wise to check beyond one bad recommendation. A friend of mine was virtually blackballed from ministry by one mean-spirited senior pastor with whom he did not get along. Everyone else thought the problem lay with the senior pastor, but it took quite a bit of research to figure that out.

Relevance

As a youth pastor, you face a unique challenge: You get older, and the kids you work with don't. We don't grow into our job, we grow out of it. Barring creative and innovative steps, we understand less and less about our charges each day.

Virtually all of you over the age of twenty-five have recognized this. And though your first clues were likely subtle ones—you noticed that it took days, not hours, to recover from a ski trip—suddenly a new kid calls you "sir" or "ma'am" and your colleagues refer to you as a "youth ministry veteran."

We actually can be remarkably better off if we navigate the transitions well. I believe the world needs a lot of thirty-, forty-, fifty-, and even sixty-somethings in youth ministry because there is no substitute for experience, maturity, and wisdom. But it's up to us to convince everyone. The first step is to stay relevant.

• **Log hang-time.** The easiest way to stay in touch with kids is to spend time with them—and the "quality time" idea is as bogus for us as it is for parents. To earn students' trust and to figure out what makes them tick, you've got to log face-time. Visit them at school. Catch their sports practice. Drop in on them at work. Visit them at home. You can learn more about a teenager by spending five minutes in his or her room than by spending two days on a retreat.

• **Read what they read.** Too many of us rely on someone else to do our thinking, especially when it comes to youth culture. And though I'll probably lose some friends with this comment, I have to say I think most of the books written about youth and sold in Christian bookstores are dated before they're printed—assuming they were accurate to begin with. If you want a current take on today's kids, read what they read. Check out the alternative press publications at the bookstore. Skim the music magazines, skateboarder rags, and any of the twenty-five look-alikes for teenage girls. And as depressing as it can be to study these publications—not to mention how embarrassing it can be to get caught reading them—they are written by people who understand today's kids.

• **Watch what they watch.** What's more informative than watching MTV? Watch and discuss MTV with students. And don't think you have to catch every inane flick targeting youth; your mind would turn to gelatin. Watch one or two, and read the reviews.

• **Ask for a critique.** Marketers are always testing their messages on focus groups, but did you know that John Stott does as well? He tests his sermons before he preaches to be sure he's connecting with people. The goal isn't to find out what people want to hear, but to find out what they hear. By asking a small group of kids to critique you and the ministry, you'll gain more insight in one hour than you could pick up from a thousand pages of reading.

- **Conduct vision trips.** Ask for a few Sundays away each year so you can visit other churches. Who's growing and why? Better yet, take a handful of adult and student leaders on a vision trip. Arrange to meet with adult and student leaders from another group for pizza and a Q-and-A format.

- **Form a personal discipleship group.** As ministries grow, we often lose contact with kids because our time is consumed with coaching adult volunteers. Stay in the trenches by maintaining a personal discipleship group. Recruit a co-leader who can pinch hit for you when upfront duties pull you away.

Resigning

Right now you are a youth pastor. A hundred years from now, you no longer will be. Between here and there lie three exit strategies. You can quit. You can be fired. Or you can die. I'm not recommending the last two, but I do have some strong feelings about option 1.

Why?

Because when it comes to quitting, which nice people refer to as "resigning," you have two options: You can do it with grace, or you can do it the way it's usually done. Those are harsh words, but not out of line with reality. Most youth ministers depart with all the grace and tact of a panzer tank.

- **The resignation letter.** In junior high you broke up by writing a note to the person you had been in "luv" with earlier in the day. In this carefully written missive, you told your luv that you didn't know how you could have ever been so stupid and that if you ever saw him or her again, you would surely barf. A courier delivered the note, and you were free to court during the next recess.

This is not the model I have in mind for a resignation letter. Instead, I'm suggesting a formal letter thanking your pastor, the board, the parents, and the youth for the chance they've given you to minister alongside them. Be gracious. Be grateful. It may have been a dreadful experience overall, but you've certainly had some good times. List them.

If you find yourself writing the letter only as an excuse to send anthrax spores in the envelope, count to a million and start again. This letter may end up in someone's file for a very long time; so if the tenor is petty, you will be remembered that way. (And when prospective employers later call for a reference, you may be chopped off at the knees.) Let me repeat myself: Resignation letters are not the place to lob bombs or list the eighteen things the church needs to change. Write a simple but gracious note, and ask a wise and trusted friend to proof it before you send it.

• **Put first things first.** Besides your spouse and one or two of your very best friends (the kind who wouldn't talk if someone was wedging bamboo shoots under their fingernails), you first need to tell the person you report to. Whatever you do, don't tell kids or parents until you've gone through the proper channels.

• **Be proactive.** Most churches handle your departure about as successfully as a one-armed man juggles chain saws. Your fans will want to throw you a world-class farewell party. Others will want to start charging you rent for every hour it takes you to get your stuff out of the church office. The two groups will wage war, and no good will come of it. So today—well before you plan to leave, so you won't seem self-serving—suggest the church standardize a policy for staff farewells—a Sunday afternoon reception with a cake and a send-off collection, for example. If everyone knows what the policy is, no time will be wasted trying to figure out how to say goodbye.

• **Give lead time.** You don't work at McDonald's, so two weeks' notice doesn't cut it. In fact, the leadership team of the church should be given as much lead time as possible to provide a smooth transition. Ideally the new hire will arrive to talk about the work a few days before you leave. If you don't get to meet face to face with the next victim, spend a few days organizing your files and writing detailed notes about upcoming events, key names, and so on. (Note: Do not leave any notes of warning about Herbert the pain. Your mother's advice was absolutely right; if you can't say something nice, don't say anything at all.)

• **Who picks your replacement?** You're the right person to make recommendations to a search committee, but you're the wrong person to be actively involved in the process.

• **Give it up.** If you resign from staff but continue to attend the church as a member, make like the invisible man. It can be done, but it'll be difficult and will require that you keep a sock in your mouth.

Retirement

Occasionally life itself or some major aspect of it becomes suddenly clear. A while back I had just such a moment when a friend said to me, "Life is so short that I'm getting pummeled by puberty and old age at the same time. My face hasn't stopped breaking out, but I'm already going bald!"

Before you know it, you will be twenty years older and facing the immediacy of retirement. Since most youth workers live—and save—like there is no tomorrow, this will not be a pleasant experience. The time to get serious about financial planning is now.

- **Objections overruled.** You undoubtedly have a handful of lame excuses about why this isn't a good idea. Let me destroy them one at a time.

Retirement isn't biblical. The Bible doesn't suggest that we shut down our ministry once we reach age sixty-two in order to live lives of leisure. In fact, it celebrates men like Caleb, who had a decade of senior citizen discounts to his credit before he begged to lead the Israelites into battle. Great point, but the wrong one. I'm not suggesting that once you hit fifty-five you deserve a thirty-year, all-expenses-paid golf outing. In fact, the idea of encouraging the people with the greatest knowledge, the broadest experience, and the widest network to drive go-carts around fancy cow pastures is loony.

But this isn't what I'm advocating. I'm arguing for stewardship. It is very likely that at some point you will be unable to work. Who will support you then? your spouse? the state? If you're not putting money away now, when you're able to pay your way, you will eventually be a burden to someone.

I don't make enough to save. "But," you stammer, "how can I save for the future when I don't make enough to live on today?" I know. Our paychecks are quickly consumed by rent, food, insurance, and other necessities too numerous to mention. However, that doesn't change the horizon. We're getting older and at some point will be unable to work. Furthermore, it has always been hard to save, but people have done it. We need to

- stop comparing ourselves with our neighbors down the street and start comparing ourselves with our neighbors around the world (we are rich), and
- develop a budget that gives back to the Lord first and puts aside money for retirement second.

It's not fun, but it can be done.

I'll rely on Social Security. A survey revealed that more Gen Xers believe in UFOs than in their likelihood of collecting Social Security, but I'll discuss this issue just in case. ("UFO Stories" by Lawrence R. Jacobs and Robert Y. Shapiro, The New Republic, from a poll done by The Third Millennium.) When our government established Social Security as a safety net, it was designed to help those who were both poor and elderly. Furthermore

- the typical American retired at sixty-five and died at seventy-one.
- during those six years, they financed life with their company pensions and personal savings and supplemented these primary sources of income with their Social Security checks.
- there were at least fifteen people adding to the pool of Social Security money for every one person taking out money.

Today those numbers have changed.

- Most people spend more time planning a two-week vacation than they spend planning for retirement, which means that we retire with virtually no personal savings to rely on.

- Medical advances have extended our lives dramatically, and early retirement has become quite common; on average, either you or your spouse will live for thirty years after retirement.
- Company pensions—for those fortunate enough to have them—aren't what they used to be.
- When the baby boomers retire, the United States will have only two people in the work force contributing to the kitty for every one person withdrawing retirement money.

It doesn't take an accountant to figure out that this dog won't hunt. If some form of Social Security is in place by the time you hit sixty-seven—note the age at which people qualify for Social Security has started to inch up—it will be reserved for those who are quite poor. You will not want to need, nor should you expect, money back from the government. Which means you will be on your own.

- **A minister's tale:** A minister we'll call John recently visited an investment broker to look into his retirement options. He's been in ministry most of his life, is now sixty years old, and would like to retire in ten years. The broker gathered the relevant information: John owns his own home, puts about $2,000 per year into an IRA, has about $100,000 set aside, and would like to have about $4,000 per month to live on in retirement. Then the broker plugged the numbers into the computer, and said, "You can retire at seventy but only if you plan to die at seventy-seven."

Imagine instead that John had made his first visit to a financial advisor when he was thirty instead of sixty. And let's also imagine that he leveraged the might of simple interest. For illustrative purposes, assume that John made $30,000 per year during his thirties, $40,000 per year during his forties, and $50,000 per year during his fifties. By putting away 10 percent of his income for thirty years instead of $2,000 for the last twenty, the results would be radically different. With a 10 percent growth rate, John would have almost $500,000 dollars today instead of $100,000. That's the power of saving.

- **The power of time:** Let me make this point one more time. Assuming that (1) we're going to retire at age sixty-five; (2) that we'll earn about 9 percent compounding interest on the money we put aside; (3) that inflation will eat away 3 percent of that nine, leaving us a 6 percent gain; and (4) that we need to replace 70 percent of our current income in order to live modestly but comfortably in retirement, then the following time line shows how important it is to start saving today.

- 25 years old: Put aside 5.2%.
- 35 years old: Put aside 10.4%.
- 45 years old: Put aside 22.7%.

• 55 years old: Put aside 64%.

• **So what are we to do?** I recommend four steps.

1. Get out of debt. The average American is financing a $5,800 balance on credit cards at the ridiculous rate of 18 to 21 percent interest. If you're making payments on any piece of plastic, you're in trouble. Take drastic steps. In fact, consider it a "sin tax" because it's wrong to be in debt or an "idiot tax" because no right-minded person would pay such usurious rates, and pay it off immediately. Cutting up your credit cards is not a bad idea.

2. Live within your means. If you can't, then something is wrong with you, your employer, or God. I'll let you wrestle with that one.

3. Ask the church to set up a 403B. Given the current tax laws, you want to put as much money into a retirement plan as you can. Furthermore, if the deposit is made automatically, you are less likely to spend it.

4. Talk with a financial advisor. There are three fundamental questions an advisor will help you answer: (1) How much should I set aside for retirement? (2) What should I do with what I set aside? (3) What should I expect from what I set aside? Ask people you trust to recommend someone they trust, and be sure to avoid all high-pressure appeals.

Finally, at the risk of undermining all I've said, take a deep breath and remind yourself that your heavenly Father cares for you and will meet your needs. Focusing too much on money and not enough on the Lord will cause wide-scale panic. That is not my goal. Forcing you to be a wise steward of your resources and to proactively face the fact that "you aren't getting any younger" is.

Road Trips

There is nothing quite like chaperoning a youth group road trip, although six years in an underground Turkish prison cell comes to mind.

Just think of it. You, four dozen adolescents and six gallons of hormones cruising down a major highway in the church van—a vehicle for which the brake pads were last changed during the Eisenhower administration. Everywhere you look there are kids. Some are sleeping, some are singing, and some are making out. Single-handedly, you are expected to drive, answer questions, read the map, and make sure everyone keeps his or her clothes on.

Lots can go wrong. Something will. You need help. That is where we'll start.

• **Help:** Because it's unlikely that you're wired to be a travel agent, you'll need to recruit additional chaperones. You might be tempted to take the first person with a valid driver's license and a van, but don't. You need a left-brained organizational wizard dying to take the entire logistical headache away from you. If you can find someone who makes lists and carries spare sets of house keys when stepping out to empty the trash, you're set. This person will be able to help you recover from every blunder.

• **Vehicles:** If you carefully study church history, you'll discover there are really only two types of churches: those who own church vans and those who do not. We'll take them one at a time.

Van rental—I've nearly killed people over rental agreements, so trust me when I say this whole business is run by the Mafia. National rental companies promise you that three twelve-passenger vans will be ready on Friday at 8 a.m.; then, when you show up, they try to substitute a station wagon, two mopeds, and a Harley Chopper with sidecar. If you plan to rent, I encourage you to go to the rental agency in person, explain that you are not open to any substitutions, and make sure the exact vehicles you need are stated in your contract. If this sounds like paranoia, it's not. Rental companies routinely overbook. They promise vehicles they don't have, and a standard rental contract will not protect you from being "upgraded" from a van to a luxury car.

Van ownership—I doubt that crash-test dummies would agree to ride in most church vans, and who could blame them? Some of these vehicles don't have jacks. Others don't have either spare tires or jacks. Others have both but no oil. Few have working brakes. I could go on, but my plea is this: Before you gas up the rusty wreck that's dripping a rainbow of fluids in the church parking lot, have a good mechanic check it out. In some cases, you're better off leaving the jalopy at home and forking out the moola to rent—especially if your trip will take you far enough away that you can't actually yell for the church secretary to send help.

• **Insurance:** Lots of people think they understand insurance. They wax eloquently about how policies transfer, who is covered by the church's plan, and whether or not the denominational umbrella policy extends to left-handed youth pastors. They sound learned, but I'm convinced most are lying. Almost no one who's cool understands this stuff, so it goes without saying that you don't. Unfortunately, you'll need to. For starters, the rental agency will try to sell you insurance for your group and a rebel army. And because half the kids' parents have threatened your life if anything goes wrong, you'll buy it. I suggest that you talk to an agent in your church before you head to the rental agency. Ask him or her to review the church's plan. Also find out what kind of coverage, if any, your drivers will need. Do they have to be twenty-one to be insured? twenty-five? Is the vehicle covered if you drive out of the country? How do you handle a claim on the road? Trust me, there's a lot to know and you'll forget most of it, so be sure to take this person's phone number with you. Which leads to the next point.

- **Phone numbers:** All carbon-based bipeds who register for the trip need to fill out a form that includes emergency phone numbers, health insurance companies, lists of medications they're allergic to, and other information too important to mention. If someone in your group is not covered by insurance or if you're heading out of the country, you might want to buy an additional primary-care policy for everyone in the group. (See "Insurance" on p. 46.)

- **CBs:** OK, I know taking CBs in a van full of teenagers—not to mention chaperones—is inviting meaningless babble for three hundred miles. But if there are fewer than four vans in a convoy, it makes good sense to stay together. Since a driver will start daydreaming and end up driving 136 mph for forty minutes, effectively leaving most of the other vehicles two states behind, you need some way to communicate. Car phones are great, but if you want to avoid the bill, try CBs. Right now several hundred of your church members probably have old CBs tucked in corners of their garages.

- **Maps:** Just for kicks, you might want to be sure that a map is in every vehicle. Some people even go so far as to make sure the maps show the right country, though those people are typically legalists. Some groups even write where they're headed each day, the phone numbers for the church or hotel where they'll stay, and the phone numbers for the other cell phones. But that is probably too much hassle. As I always say, maps are for sissies. Given enough time and gas, I can always get where I want to go.

- **Drivers:** There is more to selecting drivers than making sure they don't have a history of DWIs. I've known people who've volunteered to drive simply because they've had so many fender benders that no one in their families would let them even look at the family cars. Needless to say, this is one area where you do not ask for volunteers. We actually designed our own driving test for people who were going to operate fifteen-passenger vans. Some states require a separate license. More troubling, some states place restrictions on how many hours a chaperone may drive in a day, and you're expected to keep records in case you're stopped. (Call the highway patrol office in the states you'll be heading through.) In addition to the law, though, there are some good practices to enforce with drivers. One: They are the bosses. What a driver says goes because a stressed out, frazzled driver is an accident waiting to happen. Two: The people riding shotgun are required to pay attention to the drivers. They cannot sleep or talk to other people; their job is to make sure the drivers are alert.

- **Van keepers:** In addition to van drivers, we also appoint van keepers. These people are responsible for filling the vehicles with gas, checking the oil, and making sure the tires have air and the car top isn't about to fly off and skip down the highway. I've actually seen it happen twice—including one particularly great view out of my own rear window.

- **Rest stops:** Some people are genetically endowed with bladders the size of postage stamps. All they have to do is look at a bottle of cola, and they will have to go to the bathroom three times in the next ten minutes. (If you don't know who these people are, you will by 9:30 a.m. the first day.) The trouble is that when the group stops at a bathroom, these people are the first ones to the facilities. Then while they wait around for everyone else to go to the bathroom, they end up buying a bottle of soda. Then twenty miles later, they need to stop again. My strong advice is to find these people and take all of their change.

• **After-action report:** Finally, because whoever said that getting there was half the fun must not have been planning on having very much fun when they got there, you want to be sure to keep great records. That way, next year's travel management can be handled in half the time by any organizationally impaired idiot such as yourself. (See "After-Action Reports" on p. 9.)

Saying "Thanks"

Put this book down, walk out of your office, and start thanking people—the senior pastor, church secretary, intern, whoever. If no one is around, send e-mail messages or make calls. In fact, make it a point to say "thanks" about five or six times a day. Why? Because people respond better to praise than to punishment. And unless you're the exception to the management rule, you give neither.

And as far as thanks go, one size does not fit all. Some people thrive on compliments, while others want free T-shirts or their names in the bulletin. Take the time to figure out how each person is wired, and respond accordingly.

If you are a task-driven maniac racing toward the next goal at 100 mph, this "appreciation stuff" might be hard. But be forewarned. Your biggest fans can become your loudest critics if you don't express appreciation often enough. As a management consultant, the most bitter people I see started out as the most loyal; then as time marched on and they were taken more and more for granted, their loyalty turned to anger. Unfortunately, these people are not easily won back. They are like a bank account that is several hundred thousand dollars in the red. You can't come by and make a four-dollar deposit and expect them to be happy. You still owe $296,000 plus interest.

If you're worried you'll forget to consistently thank your volunteer army, ask a volunteer to do it. Find someone with the gift of hospitality, and put him or her in charge of quarterly appreciation nights. Or give fifty dollars to the church secretary, and ask him or her to be sure the volunteers are remembered with flowers, candy, pizza, or cab fare for their efforts. Whatever you do, remember their birthdays and anniversaries or you will be in worse shape than a goldfish doing the back float.

Seminary

"To go, or not to go?" Should you put your life on hold and pack up your books and possibly a family in order to move across the country and learn how to parse Greek verbs? Is seminary the best way to prepare for ministry?

I went—both to learn and to get my union card. Many others did not. I think I came out ahead, but that might be my own silly attempt to justify the time and money I spent. The pros and cons follow:

Pros

Seminary widened my world. Before my first day at Trinity, virtually my entire Christian life was parachurch. I had learned how to study the Bible, pray, and share my faith via Campus Crusade. But during my three years at seminary, I gained a working knowledge of missions, evangelism, church history, church polity, and counseling. I learned enough theology to suspect that a new campus ministry was a cult and enough humility to know that I needed help deciding that. I learned enough about missions to know that I was weak in that area, enough pastoral counseling to know when to refer. Mostly, I learned enough to know what questions to ask and where to go for answers.

Seminary taught me how to handle pressure. There's nothing like six thousand pages of reading, a dozen papers of "publishable" quality, and a handful of midterm and final exams to teach you how to prioritize under pressure. Though the pace occasionally made me wish I'd decided to do something easy (like law school), the workload helped prepare me for the burdens of ministry.

Seminary gave me credibility. A good friend of mine who undoubtedly knows the Bible far better than I do refuses to go to seminary because he doesn't think he should have to. He wants the system to recognize that some people are self-taught. In principle, he has a strong point. In practice, however, I'm not certain it's a battle he can win. Many jobs are simply not open to nonseminary-trained people, and they never will be.

Cons

Seminary did not teach me how to work with people. Since that's one of the most important aspects of my job, it would have been a nice skill to learn. But "people smarts" can't be taught in a classroom. If you're shy and retiring before seminary, you'll be shy, retiring, and well-read after seminary.

The problem with recent seminary graduates

"No! You cannot turn in your sermon on Monday for a slightly lower grade."

Seminary didn't prepare me for the administration monster. Hardly a word was spoken about how to organize a retreat, work with a secretary, or motivate volunteers. Those classes may have been offered, but they were decidedly second class; I was there to study the *Bible!*

Seminary did not provide me with a spiritual high. It is not a three-year spiritual retreat.

Seminary did not answer all of my theological questions. As trite as this sounds, for every question seminary answered, three new ones took its place. Things got so bad that for a while, with the exception of the deity of Christ and the authority of the Scripture, I didn't know *what* I believed.

Senior Pastors

Everybody reports to somebody, and you report to the senior pastor. Are you up to the challenge of managing him or her?

• **But I thought they managed us.** I know. You're not supposed to manage your boss. But life works better if we manage everything we can—time, money, paper, volunteers—and that includes our bosses. Obviously we can't supervise them to the extent that they supervise us. But about 25 percent of the relationship is in our court. Managing your senior pastor is about taking charge of those aspects of the relationship that are under your control.

• **Run a reality check.** This starts with expectations. Many bosses are bad news. In fact, some of the nicest people make some of the worst bosses, and that certainly applies to pastors—men and women who simply do not know how to cast vision, confront people, say no, or take charge. Or you may have the opposite problem. Your boss, a former Marine, may believe that church discipline is making you do twenty pushups every time you're late for a meeting. Finally, you may have a great boss who spends virtually no time with you. The point is that everybody has problems with his or her boss. Everybody. And the first step in making this relationship better is realizing that it never will be perfect. Headaches and hassles are part of the curse of working in a fallen world.

• **What makes them tick?** The answer lies in gathering information. Know your boss. Does he or she make the best decisions in the morning or in the afternoon? on Mondays or on Fridays? What does she love to do? What does he hate? When is the worst time to meet? When is the best time to request additional funding?

Chuck, the first senior pastor I worked for, was relaxed and affirming. We spent our time building a friendship more than a working relationship and, though we did talk shop when we needed to, he was more likely to want to discuss theology than plan the fall quarter. My second senior pastor was radically different. With David, the focus was on getting things done. We worked on five-year goals, organizational charts, and new programs. Both men served well. But the lives of the staff changed significantly from Chuck to David—and so did the way we managed them. For example, Chuck would have been insulted if I had distributed a formal agenda for our one-on-one times. David, on the other hand, thanked me for sending a meeting agenda to him the day before we met. Different people require different approaches. Know what your boss wants.

• **Keep them informed.** Recent management theory argues that supervisors should get out among the rank and file—that's us—and listen. But few senior pastors know this, and fewer have the time or inclination to do it. In good times and especially in bad times, it's in your best interest to make sure your boss knows what's going on. In fact, the worse the news or the bigger the church, the more important it is that you make sure your boss knows what's going on in your world.

Start by learning what kind of information they want. Some like to know everything about everything. Others just want to know what they have to. Learn which style your boss prefers. Also find out how they like to receive information. by phone? in a meeting? via a memo or e-mail? today? tomorrow? at next Tuesday's staff meeting? There is no right or wrong way—just their way, and you need to learn it. Then you need to take upon yourself 100 percent of the responsibility for effective communication.

• **Learn to help them help you.** Chances are your senior pastor has a wealth of experience and a truckload of information you could profit from if you knew how to tap it. Unfortunately, you must overcome two hurdles.

1. Most senior pastors suffer from the "taffy complex." So many people are making demands on their time that you simply represent one more set of sticky fingers trying to pull them in one more direction.

2. They are more important to you than you are to them. This sounds callous, but it's true. Expect them to invest far less emotional energy into their relationship with you than you do into your relationship with them. They will seldom grasp the effect they have on your emotional health and job satisfaction.

So what's the solution? Make it easy for them to help you. Carefully choose issues to discuss with them, go to them for advice only occasionally, and think through the issues beforehand so you can maximize the time. Don't dump problems in their laps; instead, frame questions. For example, instead of saying, "I don't know what to do Friday night with this gymnasium conflict," say, "The wedding reception wasn't recorded in the master calendar, and now the gym is double-booked. Their party starts at 6 p.m. and goes until 9 p.m., but I've got posters out all over town advertising an open gym and movie night starting at 8 p.m. I'm thinking about doing games in the parking lot from 8 until 9 or renting the YMCA and shuttling people over there. What would you do?"

• **Learn to help them.** Do your staff meetings run on and on without accomplishing anything? Volunteer to keep minutes so you can pull things back on track. Are you constantly fighting over who has what room when? Make a master calendar yourself. Does your boss interrupt you fifteen times before noon with ideas or comments? Offer to hold all of your questions and comments until a daily stand-up meeting, and ask for the same in return. Much of what we think is out of our control is not.

• **Compliment him or her.** The only feedback most of us get is negative. When you consider that it takes at least ten praises to balance one cut, you know that most senior pastors are functioning in a compliment deficit. A kind word from staff members helps. Compliment them for a wise decision, hard work, or good message. Take them out to lunch to say you appreciate all they do. Better yet, talk up their high points to others.

• **And in the end...** Finally, play the one trump card you have over your non-Christian counterparts. Pray for your boss. Though he or she may be incorrigible, demanding, and shortsighted, this is the person the Lord has placed over you for now. And Paul makes it clear that even slaves should pray for their masters. Ask the Lord to lighten your boss's load and bring people to the church who can help him or her serve well.

Sex

As a youth minister, you spend a good deal of your time trying to keep high school kids from doing what high school kids spend most of their time wanting to do, so I'll not keep you long. But two things are worth noting:

1. You must understand the particulars of your group. National surveys are helpful, but they shouldn't prevent you from conducting a simple, anonymous survey of your own. Use this tool to determine your students' level of sexual involvement, their understanding about the topic, and to get a grasp of what they're looking for in a boyfriend or girlfriend. Trust me, this information will go a long way toward helping you design a comprehensive plan of attack, will address their specific needs, and will shock their parents.

2. You must teach about sex. Despite what the media has led us to believe, most high school kids are pretty clueless when it comes to love and sex. They may have a biological understanding of the mating habits of frogs, many may have spent hours poring over pornography, and still others will have spent more than their fair share of time in the back seat of someone's car, but as a group they are miles away from a healthy understanding of intimacy and sexuality. So teach about sex at least once every three years. Use humor to relieve the tension, and be sure they understand that their Creator wants them to experience an exciting and dynamic sex life that's free from shame or worry.

Hold a separate session for each gender. This helps everyone feel more at ease talking about lust, masturbation, accountability, and the like. We will occasionally ask a panel of women—typically college age and older—to speak to the males in our group, and a similar panel of men to speak to the young women.

Teach about what to look for in a mate. I entitled one three-week series "How to Pick a Partner." The talks included "The Spiritual Dynamic: Why Christians Should Only Date and Marry Other Christians," "Common Sense Compatibility: What Qualities Will Really Matter in the Long Run," and "Animal Magnetism and Other Factors: Mistakes People Make in Choosing a Spouse."

Use a Q-and-A panel. Encourage people to send in their questions; then bring in a panel of two men and two women to provide as many answers as you can. The panelists should include both married and single people. It's also wise to have one person who is divorced and at least one person who did not wait until they got married to have sex.

Speak in the students' classrooms. Current high school curriculum often includes a family-life course for which students "get married," "have children," and "file for divorce" all in one week. Volunteer as an expert in the field of relationships. You may not be able to share the gospel, but your perspective will come through, and some students will seek you out after class for counseling. Additionally, many of your own students will realize that you're not as much of a drip as they'd thought.

"The Youth Pastor Speaks on Sex," as perceived by...

| The Youth | The Parents | The Senior Pastor | Himself | And in Reality |

Host a parents education workshop. Ask around until you find out which parents in your church do (or did) a good job teaching their kids about sex, and then invite those parents to speak to the other moms and dads. By equipping parents to educate their own children, you can stop a lot of problems before they start. (Besides, the parents will love you. They are desperate for help in this area.)

Stages of Ministry

Thirty-year-olds are consumed with the three M's: marriage, mortgage, and minivans. Forty-somethings are anxious about their approaching retirement and the health of their aging parents. Fifty-year-olds—if they haven't freaked out and started acting like twenty-year-olds—are either in a panic about money or are becoming quite thoughtful about life. Our own age dramatically affects our outlook. We need to be aware of how these stages of life relate to our stages of ministry.

• **One of the gang:** Many youth pastors enter ministry because they had a great time, spiritually and socially, in youth group. They may not recognize this is what they're doing—and it isn't a particularly valid "calling"—but it happens a lot. And when youth leaders with this perspective take over a youth group, several things happen: (1) they position themselves as if among equals, and (2) they schedule activities *they* enjoy—or enjoyed when they were fifteen.

When I think about my own life, I'm pretty certain this describes my first three years on a church staff. I chose college ministry because I loved college. And I dreamed of being able to hold an audience's attention like Josh McDowell. The goal is to leave this stage as early as possible for healthier models.

• **The parent model:** The next major model is the parent model, though I suppose there is something in between, where we act more like older siblings. With the parent model, your goal is no longer to keep up with the kids, but to shepherd them. (And it's likely that you have kids of your own at this point, which is part of the reason you stopped bungee jumping.) The nice thing about being an adult is you don't have to prove yourself and you inherit a certain amount of respect.

• **The grandparent model:** Sadly, few make it this far, but those who do are often worth twenty-five of their younger cousins. The white hair or complete lack of hair brings added respect not only from the kids, but also from their parents. Interestingly, Josh McDowell says he got out of youth ministry in his thirties because he was too old and got back into it in his fifties because he was older yet. Hang in there. Your day is coming.

Starting Well

Starting a new job well beats the alternatives, so let me offer a few insights.

• **Understand the power shift.** A cosmic shift occurs in your status the moment you accept a job. This shift, of course, is down. Between the time the church offers you the position and when you actually accept, you enjoy the mystical status of a celebrity. People find you wonderful, witty, and winsome. You're the dream date. Unfortunately, moments after saying, "I accept," at least a few people will start to wonder why you need the work.

Certain rules surround this power shift. Namely, you can ask for the world before you accept a job but can ask for nothing for twelve months after you sign on. Why? Because trying to renegotiate a new contract implies that your were either stupid or duplicitous when you signed the first one. So if you think you deserve a $300,000 sign-ing bonus, a Sabbatical after six weeks on the job, and first-class tickets on all mission trips, ask for them upfront. And don't try to renegotiate your contract as frequently as those who play in the NBA.

• **Act decisively.** For years we've been coached not to fix things that aren't broken and have been told the best way to start a new position is to learn the existing program. "Don't make any quick changes," people warn. "Wait a year or two to get the lay of the land." To all of this, I politely respond "bunk." Sure, it's wise to understand the

The Youth Pastor's first Sunday

"Why don't you all stand, turn to your neighbor, and tell them if you wear boxers or briefs."

program before you modify it, but two years in youth ministry is way too long to wait. Two months is pushing it. Leaders are called to lead. Walter Gerber, a senior pastor in Menlo Park, California, notes that during your first year, you have the rare opportunity to make changes. These changes need to be thoughtful and carefully articulated, but if you wait too long to act, the clay is no longer wet and will simply crack. Find the balance between riding roughshod over sacred history and moving the group forward. When in doubt, seek the counsel of parents, kids, and the senior pastor. But *do* something.

• **Study ancient and modern history.** I spent my first week as the college minister reading through old files. I was fortunate to start the job a couple of weeks before the students came back to town—a luxury you may be denied—so I had time to hide in my office and sift through the old files. By reading the minutes of old meetings, studying dated budgets, and scanning other documents, I not only learned about the previous fifteen years of student work, but I spotted trends that few others were privy to. I also learned enough about the ministry's history to ask some fairly intelligent questions.

• **Avoid first impressions.** While you're busy putting your best foot forward, understand that everyone else is as well. The first wave of contact you have with people at the church will be odd. And the truth is that many of those who go out of their way to court your favor or imply that they are power brokers are fringe players at best.

• **Get to know people.** When I was about eight years old, our church called a new minister. About three months after he arrived, he stopped by our house to visit. I'm quite sure this meeting was prearranged since our house was spotless and my brothers and sisters and I were scrubbed clean. Yet even though the evening suffered from the aura of forced spontaneity, it was good. I developed some type of bond to this man who stood behind the pulpit each Sunday morning. During your first few months in the saddle, you must make similar connections. Aggressively seek ways to hang out with both kids and parents. Learn names. Do lunch. My wife and I started one job by inviting two hundred college students to our apartment for breakfast. It was just the type of stupid idea that worked. A friend of mine attended sixty coffee gatherings in his first year at a new church. At each stop he asked, "What do you love and cherish about the church?" and "Where do you sense there may be opportunities for new approaches?"

Surviving a Full-Scale Assault

A friend of mine—we'll call him Matt—returned from a vacation to discover that he was being asked to resign. A disenfranchised former volunteer had written a letter to a member of the church board and demanded Matt's resignation.

"It was a complete surprise," he told me. He then added that the letter was not only a bombshell, but also an absolute character assassination. "In any other circle, someone would have sued."

Fortunately, cool heads prevailed, and the church brought in a denominational executive to moderate a hearing. This exec invited to a meeting all the church leaders and anyone with firsthand information to share about Matt's ministry. He made it clear that conflict is manageable if handled properly, and he instructed Matt to listen but not say anything during the meeting. The other rules were simple: No one could try to determine another person's motivation, and no one could tell someone else that he or she was wrong. What people *could* do was share different opinions.

The result? "There were good points raised about some judgment calls I'd made and also about my ability to manage anger. We also decided that a number of the problems were systemic; there was no grievance procedure for people who didn't like what I was doing. I thought people would come to me with complaints, but it turns out they are too intimidated. I didn't realize that."

Matt used the event to do some soul-searching and to look critically at his ministry. As for the critic who called for Matt's dismissal, "When the executive said you could only share criticism that was based on firsthand observations, he tore up his list and didn't say a thing."

We should expect attack—sometimes from unlikely quarters—and be prepared to deal with it judiciously. Welcome honest hearings about your performance. If the assault is unfair, others will defend you. And remember that Joseph faced some unjust busts in his day, but the Lord used it all to shape him into a real change agent. (See "Criticism—Receiving" on p. 24.)

Systems Conflict

Many of the interpersonal problems we face are caused by faulty systems. In the business world, the classic example is the tension that arises between the vice presidents of marketing and finance. The marketer always wants to spend more money on advertising, and the finance person always wants to put it in the bank. The system, as it exists, pits them against each other; consequently, before long they hate each other. In the church you might be pitted against the music minister. You want the gym for a lock-in, and he or she wants it for a citywide music festival. Before long you're each dropping subtle hints that the church's budget problems could be relieved if a "certain staff person" was sent packing. Curiously, while you might agree on what the problem is—a scheduling issue concerning the gym—you'd both be wrong. The problem is the system. Counseling sessions designed to get you to like each other do little good. Before you fix a problem, be sure you've correctly defined it. It's a lot more difficult, but ultimately more profitable, to fix the problem instead of the symptoms.

Systems Meltdown

Something else you should understand about your systems is that they melt down. Both your formal and informal procedures will only operate under certain conditions. They were created with a certain capacity in mind. When you exceed that limit, they crash. For example, you can register 10 students for a weekend retreat simply by keeping track in your head of who's coming and who has paid. When the number climbs to 25, you need to write it down. When the number climbs to 225, you need three assistants and four copies of the sign-up list. In other words, you need a new system. Generally speaking, systems break down with every 30 percent increase. If your youth group is growing rapidly, much of what you do—or at least how you do it—will need to be rethought every year.

Taking Work Home

Before you load up a briefcase, backpack, or floppy disk with a bunch of work you plan to do at home, realize four things:

1. The work won't be any more fun to do at home than it was when you didn't do it in the office.

2. Your family—if you still have one—will not be happy about this.

3. Using your off-work hours to catch up actually diminishes your efforts to get work finished during the day because you think you have an escape clause. Remove all escape clauses from your life.

4. If you take it home and don't do it, you are worse off than if you hadn't taken it home at all. Why? Because we pack expectations into the backpack, and we play a destructive mind game we're bound to lose. Our excuses follow a very predictable pattern: "I'll do this as soon as I get home" is replaced by "I'll do this right after I play with the kids." This continues all evening, and we go to work feeling far worse than we would have if we hadn't brought work home at all.

This leads me to these two rules:

1. Don't bring work home.

2. If you violate rule number one, then get the work done!

Technology

In the past fifteen years, our world has been turned sideways by the silicon chip. The chaos is likely to continue, which means that everyone over the age of twelve needs some type of proactive strategy to stay current.

• **Put mission first, hardware second.** Most of us are able to see Myst, Game Boy, and their cousins for what they are—huge black holes into which you could pour an entire week. But we are less likely to see Microsoft's latest upgrade as the same thing. Many people now do things such as generate spreadsheets or create flashy presentations just because they can, not because they need to. Define your mission first, and then figure out what tools you need. Don't let the size of your hard drive determine what your ministry looks like.

• **Embrace the change.** Those of us on the high side of thirty may have some serious computer phobias to stare down or we'll become to technology what "Pass It On" is to worship songs. Budget time and money to take periodic computer classes, or make time to read about advances in the field. Most of what is written about computers is over my head, but that doesn't apply to the technology sections in the Wall Street Journal, business publications like Forbes or Fortune, or magazines written

Even the most principled youth workers have mixed emotions about confronting certain sins.

"There, I just broke into the airline's mainframe and locked in 25 free first-class tickets for our mission trip."

for the computer hobbyist like PC World or Mac User. There are lots of ways to keep up. Follow the major trends.

• **Keep your head.** Some people have an almost total fascination with technology. We need balance. Don't allow new technology to consume you. Commit to learning, but avoid spending days at a time buried in your latest toy.

• **Adopt a nerd.** Better than learning all of this stuff from books, find a friend who can hold your hand when the machine teeters on the brink of cyber heaven. Every staff has someone who is more technically inclined than others. Seek that person out, or ask students to help. You gain an on-call expert, and he or she is given the opportunity to do something for the Kingdom.

• **Avoid first-generation hardware.** It's not uncommon for first-generation hardware and software products to have glitches, so let other people ride the outer edge of the envelope. When it's your turn to make computer purchases, buy products only after they've received a green light in the trade magazines.

To-Do Lists

Most of us carry around napkins, torn envelopes, and other scraps of paper with litanies of urgent tasks scribbled on them. The more fastidious among us recopy these lists with some frequency—being careful to add a few items we've already accomplished just so we have something to check off—and may even color-coordinate them. I'm all for lists, but there are two fatal flaws with this system: They're packed with urgent tasks but seldom with essential ones, and they're not prioritized. Your "action items" should reflect your long-term goals and create a sense of urgency for your important but not urgent tasks. Try this:

• Carry your long- and short-term goals with you at all times so they can find their way onto your prioritized to-do list.

• Glance down your list twice. The first time, put an A by the few items that matter most, a B by those that are slightly less important, a C by those that fall into the next category, and a D by those that matter the least. The second time, place an asterisk by those that are urgent. Your effectiveness will be determined by whether you focus on the A's or the asterisks.

• It might help to throw out all D's—unless some are just for fun—and to put all C's in a drawer for a month. When you pull them out, you can look to see if they have become D's, which can be thrown out, or have moved up in importance and deserve a place on your to-do list.

Once you look at your urgent tasks, you will probably get such an adrenaline buzz that you won't be able to do anything demanding reflection and careful thought. The solution: Plan at the end of the workday instead of in the morning. By spending the last fifteen minutes of the afternoon planning for the next day, you'll not only free up your early mornings for important tasks, but you'll also head home with a sense of control over the work.

Training

A friend of mine, long obsessed with the idea of making a million dollars before he turned thirty, recently confided to me that there are no shortcuts to making money. "There are lots of get-rich-quick schemes, but in the end, making money is a lot of work." Guess what? I've discovered the same thing about training volunteers. There are lots of packaged programs promising stellar results in six weeks or less, but in the end they don't deliver. Jesus spent three years with twelve people, and one still failed. Imparting skills is a tiring, one-on-one process. If you start with that assumption, you'll be a lot better off.

Which is not to suggest that training is pure drudgery. In fact, you had better make it fun and enjoyable if you want people to stay. You'd also better customize it to the specific needs of the group.

And the training had better be practical or you'll scare away all but the most loyal and bored. Seminary notes—if you have them—are a good place *not* to start. Do field work. Give your people real tools and ideas to help them hang out with students and influence them for Christ. And start with the assumption that what they need to learn are the things you know how to do intuitively. The other day I noticed that even though I've worked with students for years and still speak to large groups of them consistently, I am increasingly intimidated when I see them hanging out in small groups. Their clothes, music, hair, and tattoos make me feel like an alien. The kind of training I'd sign up for in a minute is an introduction to youth culture and one hundred ways to hang with today's kids.

Triangulation

Managing relationships is difficult enough with firsthand information. It's next to impossible with second- and third-hand stories. So don't go there. When Bobby saunters into your office and says, "I heard from Sally, who heard from Bill, who heard from Frank, that you always show up late to meetings," you need to be more worried about the rumor mill than about your reputation. For starters, you can't defend yourself against the charges without calling someone a liar.

Our legal system, for all its problems, does not operate on hearsay. Only firsthand information is allowed. My staff has agreed to the same principle. In fact, we've signed a pledge that states we will only listen to information coming straight from the source—no secondhand criticism.

Understanding People

People are even more peculiar than they look. Treat them all the same, and you'll drive everyone crazy. Spend a bit of time studying those around you, and everyone wins.

The quickest way to learn how someone is wired is to pay attention to what he or she criticizes. People usually only throw stones at things they understand. For example, I'm likely to lob a few bricks at your management style but will seldom attack your work with junior high kids. Why? I'd love to get involved with the first and would rather drink battery acid than help out with the second.

A more formal approach to determining people's skills entails using any of the assessment tools on the market. Willow Creek has done a lot with their networking program, and, if scaled down, it works quite well. Of course there are a handful of spiritual gifts surveys and at least a dozen self-scoring personality profiles. People love to take them and usually agree that they are pretty insightful. I often ask a group of people to take the test together and then to take turns guessing how everyone else scored. The drill has two advantages: The individual learns a lot about how he or she is perceived based on what people guess, and the group learns how individuals view themselves.

Vision

In the late 1980s, I asked the national leader of a parachurch group to speak at our spring retreat. After some cajoling, he agreed to pray about it, provided I would meet with him to talk about how the retreat fit into "my master plan." I suspected something was up—how many retreat speakers are this difficult to lock in?—but I wasn't prepared for what happened. After asking me a lot of questions about my ministry, my dreams, and my philosophy, he said no. "Mike, I won't speak at your retreat because I don't want to gut your ministry. You have almost no vision. Everything you're up to and thinking about is small. If I spoke at your ministry, sharing stories about what I'm up to, your best people would leave your group to follow me. I won't do that to you."

I'll leave it to you to figure out what I thought about this guy at the time—though I'll offer "arrogant," "pompous," and "conceited" as hints. But a decade later, I must admit he was onto something. Movers and shakers are attracted by visionary leaders and have little time and no patience for small-minded thinkers.

If you haven't discovered this already, you will the next time you try to recruit high-powered adult volunteers. The more successful someone is outside of the church, the bigger the vision must be to enlist him or her. Franchise players are only enticed by projects that will make a significant difference. Don't ask a person who makes million-dollar decisions all week to help you raise two hundred dollars for missions. Set your sight on two hundred thousand, and you might attract attention. Make the goal two million dollars, and he or she will either call you crazy or sign up to chair the committee. As crazy as this sounds, the bolder our plans, the more competent the people we attract.

• **Vision will make things happen.** Two years ago my staff and I completed our first five-year plan. It was exciting to have gone through the process and to have something down on paper. But the truth is that we didn't share the plan with many people because we figured they'd think we were crazy. Yet a year later when we updated the plan, we discovered that we had already achieved three-quarters of the goals we had listed. In twelve months, we had reached targets we had previously thought were risky as sixty-month ventures.

The next year brought similar results. We set significant, faith-stretching targets—goals so outlandish we again kept our vision confidential—and then watched them fall into place. Granted, it's not quite that easy. And I want to be clear: We did not reach all of our goals. But it almost seems like writing the vision on paper made it happen. It focused our prayers, attracted the right people, and generated its own energy.